THE MENTOR'S HANDBOOK

FR. PETER M. HENRY

THE
MENTOR'S
HANDBOOK

How to Form Boys into Inspiring and Capable Men

EDITED BY NATHAN ST. JOHN

FOREWORD BY ANTHONY ESOLEN

SOPHIA INSTITUTE PRESS
MANCHESTER, NEW HAMPSHIRE

Sophia Institute Press
Box 5284, Manchester, NH 03108
1-800-888-9344

www.SophiaInstitute.com

Sophia Institute Press® is a registered trademark of Sophia Institute.

Library of Congress Cataloging-in-Publication Data
Names: Henry, Peter M., author.
Title: The mentor's handbook : how to form boys into inspiring and capable
    men / Peter M. Henry ; foreword by Anthony Esolen.
Description: Manchester, New Hampshire : Sophia Institute Press, 2018. |
    Includes bibliographical references.
Identifiers: LCCN 2018028062 | ISBN 9781622826346 (pbk. : alk. paper)
Subjects: LCSH: Boys—Religious life. | Boys—Conduct of life. | Church work
    with children. | Church work—Catholic Church. | Mentoring—Religious
    aspects—Christianity.
Classification: LCC BX2347.8.B7 H46 2018 | DDC 259/.22—dc23 LC record available at https://lccn.loc.gov/2018028062

First printing

To all those who have entrusted themselves to me:
may we all know the Fatherhood of God.

CONTENTS

FOREWORD

Peter M. Henry has written the book I wish I had written, or I wish I could have written, but I concede pride of place to the master of the art. It is an old art, as old as mankind, and it is, culturally, the most dynamic art that man has ever known: it gets things done. It clears fields, builds houses, digs canals, secures food, lays down roads and highways, and flings electric wires across a continent. It goes down to the sea in ships, and down into a darker place than that, the bowels of the earth, to bring back coal and iron, copper and tin, silver and gold. It builds up the city and defends it against the wicked. The art is to turn boys into men — into a brotherhood of men united for the common good.

I hope it requires no argument to declare that boys in our time are in a bad way. They fail in school, and when they act out their frustrations, they are given psychotropic drugs, when, most of the time, hard physical work, fresh air, boyish interests, and men to teach them would clear up the problem right away. This is the sort of thing that Fr. Henry shows in his book. A boy can go to school for years and never hear, not even once, that his sex is responsible for anything other than crime, oppression, and stupidity; and nothing like that, nothing close, has ever been visited on his sisters in American public schools or Christian schools, even when it was taken for granted as a matter of social good that most girls would get married soon after high school and become homemakers with a brood of happy children. If men have succeeded remarkably at a thing—let us say, chess or epic poetry or building cathedrals or inventing machines or painting the Sistine Chapel ceiling—the boys are told that it was only because women were not permitted to do it. So all the great achievements that might move their souls are filmed over with ingratitude, if not outright slander.

Men can shrug such insults off, but boys are boys, not men, and should not have to endure it. Quite the contrary: they should be given lands to seek and realms to conquer, and if their women teachers cannot do that, or will not do it, then the education of boys must be resumed by men. That is for the sake of the boys, for the culture that will depend on their dynamism, for the women they will marry and the children they will raise. We should not fool ourselves into believing that the male sex will suddenly become utterly tame and inoffensive and compliant, when their very bodies cry out for action. There is nothing we can do about that, if not to work with nature and not against it. We understand the principle with big and energetic canines. It is only boys in our time whom, as the saying goes, we treat like dogs.

And so Fr. Henry has written an instruction manual whose every sentence speaks solid, strong, clear advice on how to make boys into men. He is a plain dealer. Boys long for the challenge, physical or spiritual or intellectual. Fr. Henry shows how to give that to them. Boys admire men who speak the truth to them and do not spare their feelings. Fr. Henry shows us how to speak the truth, not with softness, but with straight shooting and manly kindness. Boys cannot go it alone, nor have they ever done so, not in the history of the race. And so the author most wisely brings to the center of our attention what a friend of mine has called "the forgotten icon," the brotherhood, whose noblest and holiest embodiment is the band of Christ's apostles. Most moving are Fr. Henry's descriptions of what boys become for one another when a trusted man leads them and brings them out of their selfish and silly puerility. He tells a story of how one boy in his group, on a camping trip, smuggled some whiskey into the camp. Fr. Henry knew of it but did not budge from his tent. It was the boys themselves who talked turkey to their fellow, reminding him that they were on their *honor*—a word we hear very little about these days—and that Fr. Henry trusted them, and they should not betray that trust. The author recalls the silence then, and the gentle trickle of whiskey being poured out on the ground.

What about discipline? I am reminded of C. S. Lewis's shrewd observation in *The Abolition of Man*, that we remove the organ and demand the function. "We castrate, and bid the gelding be fruitful," he says. We raise up "men without chests," and then we are surprised to find that there is no honor, no spirit in the spiritual weaklings we have raised. So we now raise boys without discipline, and then we punish them for doing whatever they feel like doing. If one boy out of a class of thirty is unruly, that is his problem, though we must address it. If boys generally are unruly, then we may assume that there is no discipline at all—that is our problem. But what rewards do we reap from that discipline! We have forgotten those rewards. They are still there to be reaped, if we would but reject the lie that boys naturally and effortlessly, and without strong, clear-minded leadership from men, simply grow into their masculine nature. As Fr. Henry rightly observes:

> Men ... are not born, but made. We can no longer leave
> boys to themselves and expect them to be the type of men

who are happy and fulfilled and ready to make worthy and significant contributions to our families, our country, and our church.... Boys need to be patiently and methodically taught, nurtured and, most especially, mentored.

Now, such a statement, in the recent past, would have struck no one as controversial, neither liberal nor conservative, neither religious nor secular. It would have seemed a matter of course to the modern professor in his office just as it would to the Indian elder out on the plains. And men would readily understand the kind of mentorship needed. My father, riding from client to client in a sparsely populated region of Pennsylvania, taught my brother how to sell insurance — taught him the ropes, to use the metaphor from that masculine enterprise called sailing. He told him never to talk down the insurance that a prospective customer already had. He told him, in fact, never to bother to compare what he was selling with what a customer had already. The thing to do was to sell the policy because he believed that it was a good one and would benefit the people who bought it. He taught him how to make people *eager to take his advice*, because he showed people that he was thinking about their specific needs and was not simply out to pocket a commission. Of course, my father also taught my brother his ways, his humor, his knack for putting people at ease. My brother, I am proud to say, is one of the most successful salesmen in his company — a national company.

In other words, my father knew what to do, because he, too, had had mentors in his life. He enlisted in the army while he was waiting for my mother to be free to marry him, and he earned his sergeant's stripes in a year. He never knew enough about my intellectual interests to give me guidance that way, but he was always for me an ideal of manliness. I watched him closely. I knew when he did not like someone, because he never talked about him at all; that was his habit of never saying anything about someone unless it was good. He never used foul language. He was comfortable in his skin. He loved my mother deeply, and he worked only and always for the good of the family. He attended Mass on Sundays without fail. I learned more from him than I can express.

But many millions of boys in our time are growing up without fathers, and well-intended men themselves have no experience of what it is like to have a man for a mentor. They know that they should be leaders for their sons and for young men generally, but how to do it? A Jewish father in the time of Jesus would not have needed such directions; Joseph, I am sure, did not need them. American pioneers did not need them. We need them now, and those directions are all here, in this splendid book.

Fr. Peter Henry does far more than tell us that we should be leaders of young men, and why we should: he shows us how.

He is like a man who has rediscovered a lost art and who brings it before the attention of people who still have an instinct for beauty but have forgotten what it is or how to bring it into being. Keen is his advice, and often bracing.

He reminds us of the virtue of disinterest, meaning not "lack of care" but a healthy and manly station above personal feelings. The mentor must never congratulate himself for his successes. He must not consider them. He is a mentor not for himself and his emotional enjoyment, but for the young men, and only for them. He is more like a drill sergeant than like a pal, and, as such, he provides for the boys what they could never get from a pal.

He reminds us of the virtues, one after another, and shows how they are other or far more than we suppose. Justice is not "tolerance," which in our time usually means indifference, a slack form of injustice or spiritual sloth; justice, rather, is giving to each what is his due. Fr. Henry reminds us of courage, and, since he illustrates his points with stories, he tells of a boy who was invited to a big party and soon saw that drugs and alcohol were the main affair. The boy did not turn aside from it, pretending that it was not there. He took a deep breath, squared his shoulders, told the host that he was leaving, and walked straight out the front door, risking a great deal of ridicule. Yet many of his peers, says Fr. Henry, left the party with him.

I will conclude here with the consideration of a virtue that no one now holds forth before our boys. "Magnanimity," says Fr. Henry, "is born in man's awareness of his dignity and greatness; a realization that he was created unique and that there is no one who will follow him who will be like him. With this frame of mind, he cannot be narcissistic or self-oriented (or pusillanimous) but must always look beyond himself for the good he has yet to accomplish."

He rejects the nonsense that you can be whatever you want to be. A girl is not going to play football for the Giants. A boy who is slight of frame is not going to be a heavyweight boxer. A person of ordinary intelligence is not going to become the next Pascal or Newton.

But every one of us, because we bear the image of our divine Maker, is capable of greatness of soul: it is our birthright and our aim. We have replaced greatness of soul with correctness of politics, which is like replacing bread with sawdust, or the sun in the sky with a twenty-watt bulb in a basement. Then let the boys learn to stand straight and to aspire not to fame, that "last infirmity of noble mind," nor to fortune, which comes and goes with a spin of the wheel, but to having a soul worthy of being

a soul, of being made by God, for God, and for the rest of our
brothers and sisters in God.

Jesus was a man of great soul, on fire with love for the Father—a refining fire that would have His closest friends tried
and made pure, whether they liked it or not, and sometimes we
sense that they did not like it.

He is our example of manly tenderness and power. He does
not shrink from a duty. He does not soften the truth. He speaks
not as the endlessly citing and reciting scribes, the scholars of His
day, but with authority. He gathered a band of brothers. He made
from their very ordinary stuff the leaders of His Church—men
who would be put to the glorious death of martyrs for His truth.
So it is that Fr. Peter Henry ends his splendid book by referring
us at last to Jesus. So let me repeat the words of Jesus, to every
man who wishes to put into action the wise and strong recom-
mendations herein: "Go ye and do likewise."

THE MENTOR'S HANDBOOK

INTRODUCTION

Tecumseh was a Native American who belonged to the Shawnee people. He was a courageous warrior and a renowned leader, but never a chief. As a boy and as a young man, he roamed and hunted the lands of present-day Kentucky, Ohio, and Indiana with his surrogate father and mentor, Chiksika. Tecumseh's personal ethic and sense of justice surpassed those of many of the Americans and Europeans of his day. He despised the torture of the unarmed and respected his enemy as much as he hated him. He rejected the ways of the white man. At a time when most Native American leaders foolishly failed to understand the danger of their times, he clearly understood the consequences of the American advance into the West. He was anxious for his home, for his family, for the ancient ways of his fathers and their heritage. In the years preceding the War of 1812, he worked tirelessly to form a confederacy of Native Americans to halt the encroachment of foreigners into the lands occupied and hunted by the Shawnee and other tribes. He visited tribes as far south as present-day Florida and as far north as Canada, and he even crossed the Mississippi and traveled into the Great Plains. He carried a message, pleading with the Native American men of his time to renounce American ways, to refuse alcohol, and to return to ancient native customs. More importantly, he begged all who would listen to be ready to defend their homeland. He agonized over the plight of his people and suffered greatly for them. In the face of an obvious and overwhelmingly dangerous threat, he implored tribal leaders to join his confederacy and save their people. But Tecumseh failed.

Since my boyhood, I have felt a kinship with Tecumseh, but in no way did I ever think I was close to his equal. I have often found myself pleading with others to consider the well-being of our own people. Perhaps our current plight is not as dramatic as that which the Indian nations faced prior to the War of 1812, but it is not inconceivable that the consequences will be as dire if we do not recognize the current threat and work to eliminate it. Alas, just as many tribal leaders failed to accept Tecumseh's message and make necessary reforms, so many in our day refuse to consider the present circumstances that threaten our families. As we will discuss in this book, the male population in our society has weakened to the point at which their overall contribution to our communities may become negligible. We cannot sustain such a condition. We must collectively reconsider our current trajectory, or we will suffer the fate of the Native American who was removed from his lands and largely forgotten.

I have dedicated my adult life to building up the men who run in my circles. My goal has been to build men as husbands, fathers, Christians, and citizens—to restore individual men so that they might, again, assume the role and responsibility given them by grace and nature. As with Tecumseh, the obstacle to accomplishing this work has nearly always been the attitude of those who deny the threat and fail to see how deeply disordered and depraved our new world paradigm is. The response is always the same: a scornful review of all the failures and injustices historically associated with men and never a second thought to what men contribute. Proud of their illusionary progress, many do not see or cannot comprehend the damage that has been done. We have witnessed a long-term and consistent demise of men in our communities. Even some who hold a feminist philosophical outlook see this now. I am convinced that if we are to reverse the current trend and preserve our families, we must begin with the boys and young men among us. At the very least, they are half of the solution.

Truly, men have come to be blamed for a plethora of social ills. The irony is rich: we have abandoned our boys, failed to provide for their necessary developmental needs, and then blamed them later for being bullies, rapists, oppressors, boors, and so forth. Feminist philosopher Christina Hoff Sommers describes the situation as a "war against boys"—a phrase roundly mocked, ignored, or denied. Evidence of such a war is abundant.

My sister, a mother of girls and boys, recently shared her dismay over a favored clothing company and the blatant message they advance. The message is as inconceivable as it is obvious. The company's website advertises graphic T-shirts designed for girls and boys. Messages adorn the shirts, but the messages are inconsistent. Shirts designed for girls declare, for example, "Girls Can Do Anything"; "Girls Run the World"; "Every Girl Is a Superhero"; "Girls Never Give Up"; and "Girls Will Change the World."

The problem is certainly not with these messages. Nobody would begrudge girls support and encouragement. But the problem becomes obvious when these messages are contrasted with so many of the messages provided for boys, such as "Please Don't Make Me Do Stuff"; "Nope, I Am Going Back to Bed"; "Don't Rush Me, I'm Waiting Till the Last Minute"; "Sloth Napping Team"; and "Pizza, Sports, and Video Games."

I have no doubt that some will find such messages to be charming and will be incredulous that T-shirts will be the demise of our society. But these same people are blind to the fact that this is the message given to our boys from childhood to adulthood. The same destructive messages pervade commercials, movies, music, the classroom, colleges and universities, and even our homes. The problem is real. Consider the research completed by Mark Perry of the American Enterprise Institute: women earned 164 associate's degrees for every 100 degrees men earned; 135 bachelor's degrees for every 100 degrees men earned; 140 master's degrees for every 100 men earned; and 109 doctoral degrees for every 100 men earned.[1]

The women's movement cannot declare victory if it comes at the expense of men, and vice versa. These trends alone indicate a troubling standard that is not likely to change soon. Looking at this positively, it is obvious that the work we are doing to assist and mentor girls is, unquestionably, working. But why can we not expend the same effort and care for boys?

Since I began this work in earnest, I have had the singular privilege of assisting hundreds of young men in their quest for Christian and human excellence. My association with each of these unique young men has been an incredible experience. Some have excelled greatly; many have enjoyed considerable growth; others, perhaps the ones I appreciated the most, still look to overcome mediocrity, if not obscurity. Above all, I have tried to live the words spoken of Jesus by St. John the Baptist: "He must

---

[1] Mark Perry, "Women Earned Majority of Doctoral Degrees in 2016," *AEIdeas* (blog), September 28, 2017, http://www.aei. org/publication/women-earned-majority-of-doctoral-degrees-in-2016-for-8th-straight-year-and-outnumber-men-in-grad-school-135-to-100/.

increase, but I must decrease" (John 3:30). If I am to experience
any success with young people at all, that statement must hold
true: he must increase, and I must decrease.

That is why I offer you this book on mentoring. Although
the potential of young people is unlimited, we have cast boys
and young men aside. Worse, we are quick to criticize them and
define them according to their faults and limitations. As a result,
we, as a society, have failed to prepare the holy and virtuous men
who will inspire and guide us into the future. This is especially
true as young men's absence from church and society has been
(and will be) woefully apparent. If you see the same potential,
especially in young men; if you are pained by the neglect of them;
if you care deeply enough to consider young men with an eye to
their future, then I pray that this book will profit you—and the
young men you mentor—greatly.

Although there is an inherent satisfaction in dealing with
young people, mentors must be prepared to work. Many see
aspects of my work with young people, such as a trip to the
mountains, to be an excuse for relaxation or enjoyment, but
I consider mentoring difficult and challenging. A young man
must be frequently encouraged, challenged, corrected, and, in a
word, mentored; and such work is hard. It requires commitment,
patience, creativity, and perseverance. At times, it may feel as if
your time and effort have been wasted. Disappointment is always
a possibility, but with hard work and God's grace, the result can
be astonishing.

A word must be said about the call to greatness you will discover in these pages. The thought of pushing young men toward
greatness will be enough to fill many with anxiety. For these folks,
a call to greatness is the equivalent of a call to narcissism or a
delusional superiority. But greatness is a close imitation of Jesus

Christ—the perfect model. It requires the humble placement of one's talent, skill, and power at the service of another. Greatness guarantees right choice and requires self-mastery. Greatness can be seen in the lives of men like General Daniel Morgan of the Pennsylvania Riflemen, who saved the southern half of General Washington's Continental Army and contributed greatly to the success of the Colonies during the Revolutionary War. But it is also the tender love and protection a father affords his daughter, the love and mentoring of a man's son, or the partnership that characterizes a good and worthy marriage.

Some will respond and take up the call to greatness; others will turn an apathetic eye. This discrepancy will cause an inequality among men—some will be great while others will not—that will be unacceptable to many, and they will want it eliminated. To these, I say step aside. The time has come for good men to step forward; let us take up the work necessary to mentor great men by forging a new and healthy masculinity that will carry us into the future.

Part 1

THE CURRENT SITUATION

The Desert Father Hippolytus tells the story in the fourth century of a beautiful woman of noble birth who lived in Corinth and who had consecrated herself and her virginity to Jesus Christ. During a local persecution of Christians, the woman was arrested and taken to a pagan judge. All who encountered this woman were overwhelmed by her beauty, including the judge, who tried everything he could to seduce her. Wishing to preserve her virginity, she resisted the advances of the lustful judge, who, as a result, was driven mad with anger. He finally ordered the woman to be taken to a brothel and to work as a prostitute, earning him three coins a day. In her cell she implored God to deliver her from her circumstances and the evil men who were obviously desirous of her.

In the same city, a young man heard of the woman's reputation and the talk of her beauty as well as her arrest. That same night, he offered the jailer five coins, asking that he might stay with the woman for the entire night. The jailer agreed. When the young man entered the room, he undressed and ordered her to undress. He then quickly dressed the woman in his own clothes. He said to her, "Cover yourself completely with the tunic and get out of here." The woman, sealing herself with the Sign of the Cross, quietly walked out of her cell, past the jailer, and out of the prison with her virginity intact.

The next day, when the young man's intervention was discovered, he was ordered to appear before the judge, who sent him to the amphitheater to be killed by wild beasts.[2]

I have told this story to countless young men, and it always receives the same reaction. The young men, no matter who they are or what their circumstances, are physically and emotionally moved. You can see it in their faces: they long to be the hero in the story; they were born to be the hero in the story. They do not want to be a hero in the narcissistic "see my greatness" sense, but in an authentic, selfless-love sort of way, a love imitating the Crucified One. Even as the name of this young hero, a martyr for the Faith and a martyr for purity, is unknown to us, young men know him to have succeeded. They admire him even as they, too, long to succeed in much the same way. Perhaps their success will not entail such intense, inspiring drama, but they are made for the same heroic virtue exhibited by this young nameless man centuries ago.

As we will see later in this book, men are generally not born with such virtue. A mentor directs his attention to a boy with the intention of helping him achieve this courageous ideal. A boy is chosen and taught and must be convinced that this ideal is real and that he can and will achieve this greatness in time. Men, some young and some old, who exhibit poor or even ridiculous behavior today, surround us. Some people, with great smugness, condemn men as animalistic and hold to an anti-male prejudice or stereotype. The fact is, if a young man fails today, it is because

---

[2] Robert Meyer, trans., *Palladius: The Lausiac History* (New York: Paulist Press, 1964).

we have failed him first. Proper mentoring and character development are all that is necessary to bring heroic acts of virtue to the foreground. But this is a message a young man may never hear today; in fact, he very likely knows the opposite: he knows that by all counts and measures, he and his brothers are in trouble.

Boys are awash in a quagmire of competing social agendas and widespread cultural confusion. As controversial as it may sound, we have taken everything away that boys need for proper maturity and development, and then we make them the object of scorn and ridicule when they fail. Society has experienced radical change in the past century; boys and young men have been pushed to the side and corporately neglected. "Adapt or die" has become the mantra of social engineers who have betrayed our human nature for an artificial society designed to implement their own worldview. Surely, boys and young men are failing, but the task set before them is impossible. The task is akin to making a bird swim like a fish in water. The bird, having been required to do something contrary to its nature, will return to the surface after failing and, as a result, will be angry and utterly frustrated. As a bluegrass band composed of young men sings, "There ain't no use in trying anymore."

To be sure, men have not lost their power (any more than women have). The 170,000 years of natural evolution that formed *Homo sapiens* males into what they are today will not pass in one generation. Men are endowed by nature with a certain amount of raw power that, from the beginning, was to be used for the good of humanity. What has been lost, however, is opportunity: opportunity to be positively mentored and instructed in proper masculine identity and to use personal power for the good of others. In fact, the opportunity to serve the community in chiefly masculine roles is disappearing. Highly qualified men (soldiers, for

example, whose bodies have specifically evolved for protection
and defense) are told to step aside, as men are no longer valued
as a vital part of the community, especially in the United States
and Europe. The prominent idea that men are losing their power
and, as a result, are reacting badly is a non sequitur, as boys are
not even given a chance today. Boys will grow up to be men.
With manhood comes great responsibility. We have a choice:
either equip boys to become virtuous, well-adjusted, self-mastered
men, or suffer unimaginable consequences.

Women were the first to bring all of this to my attention.
When I was a newly ordained priest and encountered women
outside the confessional or in my parish office, the problem became clear. Over and over, women would complain about the
men in their lives — whether spouses, fiancés, or boyfriends. The
situation was pandemic. A married woman would often complain
about her husband's immature character, his apathetic approach
to life, his lack of self-confidence, his disregard for his offspring,
his general disinterest in building a career, his discontentment,
and his undependability. Unmarried women, searching for worthy
partners with whom they might spend their lives, complained
about men who played video games, smoked pot, could not hold
a job or graduate from college, pressed them for illicit sex or
sexual activity, or, generally speaking, were not worth the time
and energy these women had invested in them.

And even though some refuse to admit there is a problem,
the situation described above has become exceedingly dangerous to the future and security of our families, our country, and
civilization itself. More than likely, social engineers (by which
we mean those not satisfied with the natural order, who seek to
reorder the world according to their subjective ideas) will scoff
at the notion that the rejection of traditional gender roles and

the remaking of societal norms has or will cause problems. History, surely, will prove them to have been exceedingly mistaken and extraordinarily irresponsible. Even so, today we seem to be entering a new era of hope. After many years, pundits and social commentators are finally acknowledging, if ever so cautiously, the dismal situation of men and the negative impact the situation has had on our society. Studies and statistics are increasingly sounding the alarm that the male population is in dire trouble.[3] From many quarters, including some feminist quarters,[4] many are anxious about our situation.

[3]   See Michael Keating, "The Strange Case of the Self-Dwarfing Man: Modernity, Magnanimity, and Thomas Aquinas," *Logos: A Journal of Catholic Thought and Culture* 10, no. 4 (2007): 55–76; Matthew J. Christoff, *The Catholic "Man-Crisis" Fact Sheet*, The New Evangelization, July 7, 2015, http://www.newemangeliza-tion.com/man-crisis/the-catholic-man-crisis-factsheet/; David French, "On Man's Duty to Defend the Weak and Vulnerable," *National Review*, July 15, 2015, http://www.nationalreview.com/article/421227/mans-duty-defend-weak-and-vulnerable-david-french; Congressional Budget Office, *Trends in the Joblessness and Incarceration of Young Men*, Congressional Budget Office, May 9, 2016, http://www.cbo.gov/publication/51495; Jonathan Vespa, *The Changing Economics and Demographics of Young Adulthood: 1975–2016*, publication No. P20-579 (Washington, D.C.: United States Census Bureau, 2017), https://www.census.gov/content/dam/Census/library/publications/2017/demo/p20-579.pdf; Thomas B. Edsall, "The Increasing Significance of the Decline of Men," *New York Times*, March 16, 2017; Young Warriors, "At-Risk Boys Become At-Risk Men," Young Warriors, https://www.youngwarriors.org/for-parents-teachers/at-risk/.

[4]   Christina Hoff Sommers, *The War Against Boys: How Misguided Policies Are Harming Our Young Men* (New York: Simon and Schuster, 2013); Kay S. Hymowitz, *Manning Up: How the Rise of Women Has Turned Men into Boys* (New York: Basic Books, 2012).

Educator, author, and public speaker James Stenson, co-founder of the Heights School in suburban Washington, D.C., and founder and first headmaster of Northridge Preparatory School in suburban Chicago, confirms this worrisome outlook:

> We look around in our workplaces and neighborhoods and see young people in their 20's who are immature and irresolute, soft and irresponsible, uneasy about themselves and their futures. They may be technically skilled in some field and hold down decently paying jobs, but their personal lives and marriages are a wreck. In their conduct and attitudes, these young people seem permanently stuck in adolescence, that dangerous mixture of adult powers and childlike irresponsibility. Some are crippled or destroyed by substance abuse. But even if they remain drug-free (what a strange term!), many see their professional work as mere ego gratification or (an adolescent attitude) just drudgery endured for the sake of "spending money." Great numbers of them live as heartless narcissists, caring little or nothing about their parents or their children, if they choose to have any. They retain within themselves, sometimes tragically, the flawed attitudes and habits of childhood. For some reason, they never quite grew up.[5]

Nonetheless, it is one thing to admit there is a problem and quite another to know what to do about it. And, as I have taught for many years, the problem can be solved only by men willing to do the work necessary to mentor their sons and younger brothers

---

[5] James Stenson, "Danger Signs: Families Headed for Trouble," Catholic Parents OnLine, 2005, https://www.catholicparents.org/danger-signs-families-headed-trouble/.

and reverse the current trends. But this also raises difficulties. The skill of mentoring has nearly disappeared in our society. In the recent past, boys learned to become men by working alongside their fathers, older brothers, uncles, and grandfathers. They learned honesty, hard work, virtue, character, and their place in the world in a very natural manner: by living or dying by the success of their fathers and their fathers' businesses or family farms. Men would work and sweat together, fulfilling an important role for the family and the community in which they lived. They enjoyed an unspoken intimacy—a one-on-one, or "iron sharpens iron" (Prov. 27:17), relationship; a mentoring that was more of action than of words.

Then everything changed.

In the later part of the nineteenth century, men began leaving the small shops and farms and entered the hard, cold world of the industrial revolution. For the first time, fathers were separated from their children for at least eight hours a day. And when the fire of the revolution became hot, time away from sons and daughters increased rapidly. The situation would become even worse, with men pursuing careers or fighting foreign wars. Fathers saw less of their sons and, to great disadvantage, became ever more estranged from them. The result was devastating and led to the immaturity and foolishness of the culturally celebrated sixties generation with their sexual revolution, drug and divorce culture, and rejection of all things tried and traditional.

All of this produced a profound disconnect between men and their children, especially their sons. I speak in somewhat general terms, but anyone with the power of observation can see that things can be much better than they are. Young men are under the spell of pornography, drugs, mediocrity, social media, Netflix, and video games. They seek meaning, fulfillment, and affirmation in violence, materialism, and illicit sexual activity. They do not seem capable of aspiring, and few are interested in or excited about their future. All of this results in what I consider one of the most grievous aspects of the current man disaster: the inability of a boy to know and embrace his true potential and stand in the glorious realm of the men who have gone before him.

Again, these modern trends and circumstances can be reversed. A young lady can find a good man who is her equal and with whom she can happily share her life. Our boys can find meaning and purpose. Our communities, once again, can be healthy and strong. Boys and young men can be empowered to realize their natural and divinely decreed vocation to provide and protect once again. All of this can easily be accomplished when good and generous men — like you — begin to rediscover the ancient, natural, and essential art of mentoring.

A Young Man's Self-Image: Why It Is Alarming and How It Will Be Changed

Growing up in America in the last five decades has proven to be extremely dangerous to boys and young men. One has only to consider the endless diet of harmful Hollywood nonsense that is ever present to young people (if even subliminally). Contrast Michelangelo's sixteenth-century image of David with the main character in Paul and Chris Weitz's infamous movie *American Pie* (1999). Michelangelo carved an image of David that reflects the platonic form of man: self-mastered, self-confident, at ease in any situation, looking beyond himself, ready to accept any forthcoming challenge—a powerful force with which to be reckoned. On the other hand, the Weitzes gave us a contemptible movie (seen by hundreds of thousands of young people), in which the main character is led to believe that "third base" is like "warm apple pie," and so the young man seeks to experience sexual intimacy—something that should be held as sacred and privileged—by attempting intercourse with a pie. The directors liken the title of the movie to the "quest of losing one's virginity in high school," which they maintain is "as American as apple pie." Harmless and innocent humor? No wonder young men have come to view themselves as filthy, shameful, dangerous, and untrustworthy. Anyone with the ability to reason ought to draw worrisome conclusions about young men and their self-perception today. *American Pie* is just one example of a host of vile propaganda to which young men have been exposed. Is it any wonder that our daughters are not safe, even while on a college campus of "higher learning"?

For years, I have wondered about the motivation of movie producers. Pardon the example, but how many times have we seen, in so-called comedies, the now obligatory "crotch shot" when a man doubles over in pain after being struck in his groin? This often elicits awkward laughter from viewers. But why? The argument can be made that Hollywood producers are revealing a vile contempt for the human male. And, of course, it does not stop here; contempt for all sexuality is a common theme for the entertainment industry. For the past three or four decades, propagators of print media, theater, movies, education, and marketing have used their venue in an attempt to reorder society to fit their own worldview, which holds thousands of years of social interaction and human development in complete disdain. In countless television programs and videos and an overwhelming number of commercials, men are portrayed as incapable buffoons. In commercial television and videos, women are required to show men around hardware stores, demonstrate how to drive sports cars, and explain how to run multimillion-dollar businesses and corporations, not to mention the workings of family life. The entertainment industry portrays young men as concerned about one thing: illicit and uncommitted sex.

The gender-equality misconception is oftentimes subtle and crafty. Movies often portray petite beautiful women as powerful forces capable of hand-to-hand combat and dominance of men. They also portray women in unconventional roles, such as military commanders, commandos, and even powerful villains. I am not suggesting that women cannot hold these positions, but it is a stretch to claim that such media is "art imitating life," as its producers are so fond of saying. Rather, what we see is art instructing men in how they are to live and think about themselves and what place they are to hold in this new world. We have arrived at the point, as one sociologist has indicated, at which men must change or face the end of men.[6]

Unfortunately, our society has become very hostile toward boys and young men. A lifetime of Hollywood productions, music lyrics, news programs, liberal education, pornography, and video games has taught young men that they are the problem rather than the solution. As is accepted and often repeated, the most dangerous animal on the planet is the adolescent male. A young man growing up is continuously and often subliminally taught by those in his own neighborhood that he is lazy, stupid, prone to violence, inept, lacking ambition, and completely given over to a troubling and grotesque thirst for sex.

Disagree? What goes through the mind of a young man when he first arrives on a college campus and is required to attend a conference on "sexual consent" or "date rape"?[7] Or recall the

---

6   Hannah Rosin, *The End of Men: And the Rise of Women* (New York: Riverhead Books, 2012).

7   Duke Women's Center, Duke Men's Project, Facebook page, https://www.facebook.com/pg/DukeMensProject/about/?ref= page_internal; Andrew Hahn, "New Campus Program Asks, 'What Is Masculinity?'" University of Wisconsin–Madison, University Health Services, https://www.uhs.wisc.edu/news/ campus/mens-project/; Toni Airaksinen, "Princeton's New

great achievement of the Obama administration that allowed a young person to remain on his parents' health insurance until the age of twenty-six. That is success? On the contrary, economic liberty and parental independence should manifest themselves much earlier than the age of twenty-six. Even families ordered to the growth and development of their children cannot prevent their sons from hearing these denunciations of themselves and their male peers. They even hear these denunciations in the classroom. Under the term "patriarchy," which is always used pejoratively, boys are taught that women have been oppressed for centuries as the result of the success of men and the contributions they have made to society. Consequently, young men are pushed aside and deliberately neglected in order that social engineers might achieve an artificial restructuring of the social order.

As difficult as it may be for some to consider, divorce has also had an incredibly negative impact on both boys and girls. Of course, divorced parents do not want to believe their situation has adversely affected their children, but the destructive force of divorce on the lives of children must be acknowledged and addressed. I have known several cases of junior high school boys who, faced with their parents' divorce and the perceived failure of their fathers, have, in their anger, hurt, and confusion, turned to viewing homosexual pornography—something they never

---

'Men's Engagement Manager' to Combat Aggressive Masculinity on Campus," The College Fix, July 25, 2017, https://www.thecollegefix.com/post/34858/; Olivia Campbell, "The Men Taking Classes to Unlearn Toxic Masculinity," *The Cut*, October 23, 2017, https://www.thecut.com/2017/10/the-men-taking-classes-to-unlearn-toxic-masculinity.html.

had imagined doing. They cannot tell you why or articulate what they are seeking in such a pursuit, but they nevertheless pursue this destructive behavior—so unsettling is the crumbling of a child's world. This is but one example of many. A review of recent studies will confirm that boys are falling behind girls in education;[8] they are increasingly becoming addicted to pornography;[9] they will admit to perpetrating sexual violence;[10] they cannot meet basic physical and psychological standards to enter the military;[11] they are more increasingly unemployed with fewer career prospects;[12] they have less and less interest in marriage;[13] they suffer from a lack of self-confidence;[14] they are

[8] Jeff Sossamon, "Girls Lead Boys in Academic Achievement Globally," News Bureau, University of Missouri–Columbia, January 26, 2015, http://munews.missouri.edu/news-releases/2015/0126-girls-lead-boys-in-academic-achievement-globally/.

[9] Wendy Maltz, "Pornography on the Rise: A Growing Mental Health Problem." *Psychotherapy Networker*, November 11, 2015, https://www.psychotherapynetworker.org/blog/details/677/pornography-on-the-rise-a-growing-mental-health-problem.

[10] Gabrielle Noone, "38 Percent of College Men Admit to Coercing Women into Sex, according to a New Study," *New York Magazine* (June 2016).

[11] Andrew Tilghman, "The Military May Relax Recruiting Standards for Fitness and Pot Use," *Military Times*, November 1, 2016.

[12] Congressional Budget Office, *Trends in the Joblessness and Incarceration of Young Men* (Washington, D.C.: Congressional Budget Office, 2016), http://www.cbo.gov/publication/51495.

[13] Meg Murphy, "NowUKnow: Why Millennials Refuse to Get Married," Bentley University, 2017, https://www.bentley.edu/impact/articles/nowuknow-why-millennials-refuse-get-married.

[14] Kyle Smith, "Life in the Childish States of America," *New York Post*, May 29, 2016, https://nypost.com/2016/05/29/life-in-the-childish-states-of-america/.

sexually addicted and gender confused;[15] and they are more apt to commit suicide.[16]

Men, including the young, have complained for decades that the modern world has pressured them to conform to unnatural norms, to be socially domesticated, and to forgo any semblance of an authentic masculine identity. By "authentic masculine identity," I do not mean a version of man typified by sitting on a couch, drinking beer, eating pork rinds, and watching television. Men need to believe in themselves and strive to reach their higher selves.

Once again, however, the culture has an alternative agenda. Jennifer Siebel Newsom has been working for several years on a video documentary that social engineers have celebrated. To fund her project, she solicited funds from Kickstarter, using the following pitch:

> At a young age, boys learn that to express compassion or empathy is to show weakness. They hear confusing messages that force them to repress their emotions, establish hierarchies, and constantly prove their masculinity. They often feel compelled to abide by a rigid code of conduct that affects their relationships, narrows their definition of success and, in some cases, leads to acts of violence

[15] Melissa Olivas, Nikki Liu, and Lauren Wallitsch, "The Study of Men and Sexual Addictions," *Psychology of Men* (Fall 2008), https://psychofmen.wordpress.com/final-papers/the-study-of-men-and-sexual-addictions/.

[16] Sally C. Curtin, Margaret Warner, and Holly Hedegaard, *Suicide Rates for Females and Males by Race and Ethnicity: United States, 1999 and 2014* (Washington, D.C.: National Center for Health Statistics, 2016), https://www.cdc.gov/nchs/data/hestat/suicide/rates_1999_2014.pdf.

resulting in what many researchers call a "boy crisis." Our society's failure to recognize and care for the social and emotional well-being of our boys contributes to a nation of young men who navigate adversity and conflict with an incomplete emotional skill set. Whether boys and later men have chosen to resist or conform to this masculine norm, there is loneliness, anxiety, and pain.[17]

Nobody will question Newsom's desire to improve the situation of people in our world. Her sincerity and hard work to discover solutions and apply remedies is admirable. But it must be frankly stated that her analysis is questionable, as her suggested solutions contribute directly to the problem! Unfortunately, she does not understand the male psyche and will succeed only in causing more confusion, resentment, and difficulties. This is very important and must be properly understood. Let us break down her statement to understand the implications.

"At a young age, boys learn that to express compassion or empathy is to show weakness." This statement is dubious at best. Data supporting this statement would be nearly impossible to collect. As a former boy raised in a Christian family, I can safely assert that I was never once taught that to show empathy is to show weakness. Newsom is making a fundamental mistake made by most social engineers. She assumes that, for boys to be healthy, they ought to act and behave in the manner that girls act and behave. No matter how much social engineers protest, girls are nurturers and are naturally sympathetic. Who would expect boys, biologically destined to be protectors and defenders,

---

[17] Jennifer Siebel Newsom, "The Mask You Live In," Kickstarter, "Why This Film Matters" section, http://www.kickstarter.com/projects/jensiebelnewsom/the-mask-you-live-in.

to express affective empathy or compassion? Boys long to be heroes—to rescue and save. Does this not imply empathy? Risking one's life to save another from some calamity is empathy in action, empathy in masculine form. In other words, both men and women are or can be empathetic, but rarely in the same way. To tell a boy he must emote in the way girls do is to imply there is something wrong with him—a message he will hear often as he grows up.

"They hear confusing messages that force them to repress their emotions." Newsom is making another assumption here. Perhaps it has never occurred to her that men seldom find the need to cry. To tell a man that he must cry to express his emotional well-being, even when he does not see the need, is frustrating. Truthfully, if left alone, a man can easily express emotion. But pressuring a man to "express his feelings" will do the opposite: it will cause him to suppress his emotions. As a spiritual father, I have found that when a man feels the need to cry in my presence, he often feels free to do so. But he is never told to do so! I recall praising a man for the great job he did in raising his son; he freely and without shame cried tears of love before me. Others cry when discussing their fathers; many cry as the result of relational difficulties with women; still others when faced with very difficult or troubling situations. Sure, women express emotion more openly, even in a group setting, but such a setting would often be the wrong context for a man.

Ironically, few women would be attracted to a man who exhibited such lack of self-control, and men know it. Why women like Newsom insist on adapting the behavioral patterns of men is perplexing. In the proper setting, boys and men have little problem expressing themselves. But to force a reaction or to be told it must be done in a certain way (to the satisfaction of others) will serve only to make a boy or a young man feel inadequate and foolish.

"They hear confusing messages that force them to ... establish hierarchies and constantly prove their masculinity." The establishment of hierarchies might sound frightening to some and has even been completely condemned by the feminist movement, but hierarchy is a source of confidence and inclusion for boys and men. Males have established productive hierarchies for centuries: they involve teamwork and allow boys and men to accomplish important tasks. True, a boy can feel terrible when he does not make the cut and finds himself outside the hierarchy, but the discovery of this inadequacy often prompts him to work harder to measure up. This serves to make him a better man. Boys and men receive much affirmation and even love by belonging to a hierarchy or a fraternity. The key is to ensure that these hierarchies are motivated by positive, productive goals. Consider organized sports, the Knights of Columbus, and the priesthood—all positive and hierarchical. Why would Newsom want to deprive a boy or a young man of such an important and formative experience?

It is true that men feel compelled to "prove their masculinity." When a boy or a man can effectively interact on a work project or be part of a team in an athletic event and thus prove himself, he can happily put that anxiety to rest. On the other hand, a man who has never had the opportunity to prove his masculinity to himself or to other men will be consigned to questioning his worth as a man. That might sound okay to some, but not to men who are not afraid of a challenge and are able, following a defeat, to regroup and give it another try. The test that accompanies acceptance by other men is necessary, and a world without this test would be pointless to a man. Once he has passed this test, he is integrated into the group and within himself. It is an uninitiated man, or a man who is never afforded the chance to prove himself, who is certainly a miserable man.

"They often feel compelled to abide by a rigid code of conduct that affects their relationships, narrows their definition of success and, in some cases, leads to acts of violence resulting in what many researchers call a 'boy crisis.'" Surely men will and do hold each other to a rigid code of conduct. The code is important but may not be what some suggest. A good code clearly states: "You shall not harm your wife or girlfriend, but rather, shall honor, cherish, and respect her; you will be a man of your word; you will work hard and pull your own weight; you will never steal; you will not leave a brother behind; you will exhibit purity of action, decency in speech, respect toward others; you will be known for a good-natured spirit." If men are allowed to teach this code to their sons and brothers, men will overcome their propensity to brutishness. Which part of this "rigid code" would Newsom like to eliminate?

Whether boys and men choose to resist or conform to an authentic masculine norm will determine whether they live happily or in loneliness, anxiety, and pain.

Recently, I watched a cable news talk show that invited a male psychologist to discuss men's issues in an open forum. The psychologist opened his remarks by cheerfully announcing that men must be "handled" and "managed" and that the best way to do so is to consider them as "four-year-olds who know how to shave." But why leave men with such an image of themselves?

In addition, I have listened to many people discuss issues of concern to men. Most speakers open their remarks with a lengthy bit of mockery and joking. Even proponents of men and masculine virtue cannot resist the temptation to mock and belittle men and fathers. If a young man overheard these statements and positions, why would he strive to make the best of his life and to contribute to the welfare of us all? We succeed only in giving men permission to be mediocre and irrelevant.

But how might boys and young men think about themselves? As the world fumbles along in confusion, let us look to a profound model for the character of a man: Jesus Christ. To do so, consider a passage from Sacred Scripture:

> [Pilate] went out to the Jews again, and told them, "I find no crime in him. But you have a custom that I should release one man for you at the Passover; will you have me release for you the King of the Jews?" They cried out again, "Not this man, but Barabbas!"... Then Pilate took Jesus and scourged him.... So Jesus came out, wearing the crown of thorns and the purple robe. Pilate said to them, "Here is the man!" When the chief priests and the officers saw him, they cried out, "Crucify him, crucify him!" (John 18:39–19:5)

To understand the magnitude of what is happening here, one must understand the expectations of the Jewish people toward Jesus. The Jews were anticipating the arrival of a military messiah at the time of Jesus. They had suffered greatly under the oppression of the Roman Empire and believed that a military messiah would lead a revolt powerful enough to restore the Davidic Kingdom and secure their freedom. When Jesus appears before the Jews, He does so under the weight of their heavy expectations. That is why He enters Jerusalem as a Messianic King and a week later the Jews want Him crucified. Have you ever wondered why St. Peter was in the garden with Jesus to pray and was wielding a sword?

So Pilate unwittingly places before us a choice: "Behold the man!" On his right hand stands Jesus—a man who had incredible power that He did not conceal. He was able to feed five thousand people with a mere basket of bread and some fish (John 6:1–11). Consider the usefulness of such power in the hands of a military leader. Jesus also had the power to cure the blind, lepers, paralytics, and even Malchus, the slave whose ear St. Peter severed when Jesus was arrested. In the course of battle, who would overlook the usefulness of this skill? More importantly, Jesus had power over death, raising his friend Lazarus, who had died three days earlier (John 11:1–44), a widow's son (Luke 7:11–17), and the daughter of Jairus (Mark 5:35–43). With this kind of power, a military leader could restore dead soldiers quickly to the battlefield. And how many times have military campaigns been decided by the uncontrollable elements of nature? Yet Jesus had powers applicable here as well. He could walk on water (John 6:16–21), calm storms (Mark 4:35–41), curse a fig tree to its doom (Mark 11:12–14), and provide a miraculous catch of fish (Luke 5:1–11). Based on this brief résumé of Christ's power and abilities, even a Roman general would think twice before engaging such a leader in battle.

Nonetheless, Jesus offers little expectation of a military rebellion. We see this when we witness His daily routine: "And in the morning ... he rose and went out to a lonely place, and there he prayed.... And he went throughout all Galilee, preaching in their synagogues and casting out demons. And a leper came to him beseeching him, and ... he stretched out his hand and touched him.... And immediately the leprosy left him" (Mark 1:35, 39, 40–42).

On Pilate's left hand is Barabbas, whose name in Aramaic, ironically (if not sarcastically), means "son of the father" — a title more appropriate for Jesus. Barabbas, unlike the way he is portrayed in Mel Gibson's *The Passion of the Christ* (2004), is not a lunatic. He is a leader, a man of action, and a man who could offer hope to Israel. He is tough, bold, and cruel. Scripture describes him as a man who "committed murder in the insurrection" (Mark 15:7) and as "a notorious prisoner" (Matt. 27:16) and "a robber" (John 18:40).

Reflecting on this scene from Scripture, we can draw some important conclusions. First, all men are undeniably endowed by God with significant personal power. In the objective world of nature, that cannot be denied. Evolution has manipulated man's body to be a machine for the defense and care of his family; his body certainly bespeaks the condition of a warrior and a provider. Even more, men who are husbands and fathers have an enormous influence over the emotional and psychological well-being of their wives and families. Men are natural-born leaders, builders, and dreamers. Ultimately, men are generative. A man should celebrate and respect all of this.

Secondly, man is given the freedom to choose the type of man he will be and what he will do with the power he has been given. It would be wrong, in the spiritual realm, for a man to lay claim to this power exclusively for his own benefit; after all, he is but a custodian of this power, "for there is no authority except from God" (Rom. 13:1). But God has given man, from Adam to modern man, the freedom to choose the type of custodian he will be.

Will he be like Barabbas: selfish, narcissistic, opportunistic, lusting for greater power and dominance? Or will he be like Jesus: eager to use what he has been given for the benefit of others—family, friends, community, and country? Every man makes his choice, or rather, is required to make his choice. Jesus makes the correct choice, as is plainly evident by His life. Power is intended to be used for others: "Let us love one another" (1

John 4:7). Remarkably, God lets each man decide how he will use his power. For a very long time now, boys and young men have not been given opportunities to strive for greatness (which encompasses man's use of power), and they may not even be aware of the possibilities. But today, when a young man fails or goes on a violent rampage, naysayers point their fingers and wag their heads.

A core necessity for any person, male or female, is his identity. In years past, a boy was raised as a part of a community. He knew who he was because he knew from where and from whom he had come. His family, his community, his country, and his faith informed him about who he was.

Many are surprised to learn that an initial step in establishing socialism is to separate sons from their fathers. That way, the individual's identity can be redefined or remade. This philosophy has pervaded our society and can be seen everywhere. Even the United States Supreme Court has accepted and even encourages this new way of thinking: a person, so they wrote, has "the right to define one's own concept of existence, of meaning, of the universe, and of the mystery of human life" (*Planned Parenthood v. Casey*, 1992), and again, we are granted "specific rights that allow persons, within a lawful realm, to define and express their identity" (*Obergefell v. Hodges*, 2015). It is hard to believe that highly educated, intelligent people can be so shallow and misinformed. Whereas some may find culture and heritage an oppressive human limitation, others know that our heritage, culture, history, and faith form a dependable and necessary foundation without which personal happiness and productive living are impossible.

But this is exactly what we have done to our boys and young men: we have left them rudderless under the influence of a depraved culture. Absent is a profound humility before the Fatherhood of God and of His creation. Absent is an acknowledgment of man's nature, not as a restriction of our freedom or oppression of the individual, but, rather, as a cosmic guide directed toward the true purpose of man and woman.

Mankind has thrived on the planet for countless generations. An ancient wisdom infused with grace formed mankind and now shows humanity that which is best and most effective for stability, security, and earthly happiness. In the wisdom of God, all men and women are granted equality, but in the wisdom of nature, all have been given different and important roles to fulfill. We ignore this truth to our peril.

Hope prevails. Talk to young men and boys: with very few exceptions, they still intuitively know they are meant for higher ideals, great feats of selfless sacrifice, and heroic lives of virtue and honor. They crave the greater, the sacred things in life. These ideals remain latent in the heart of young men. The mentor must wade through the sewage of a corrupt, disturbing culture, tap the imagination of his young disciple, and help him realize the truth about himself. He must convince his disciple that he need not be lazy, unmotivated, fixated on illicit sex, boorish, and destined to a life of video games in the basement of his mother's house. Nor should he be reconciled to this plight. More than anything else, a young man yearns to be challenged to be something greater than he is, and he will very likely respond to the challenge of excellence with enthusiasm and determination.

I invite you to sit with a young man and allow him to share with you his innermost thoughts, feelings, anxieties, and motivations. If you are patient and eager to listen, you will discover in him, without any exception, a good man who very much desires to be better.

2

UNREALIZED POTENTIAL: WHAT HAS CAUSED MEN TO SURRENDER?

I was not prepared when a young man approached me at a major university and stood squarely before me. He questioned me before he even greeted me: "Father, do you know why we appreciate you?" Now, before you think poorly of me, you must realize that I was stunned by his question, probably because my family rarely, if ever, talked of unspeakable things like affirmation. "Uh, no," I muttered back. Without delay, he asserted, "Because you challenge us to be better than we are." Although it is always satisfying to be appreciated, the young man's statement troubled me deeply. Young men know intuitively that they are not reaching their potential.

There is nothing more discouraging than to encounter a truly blessed young man — and most of them are — and realize that he is not the man God has created him to be. The prophet Samuel had some rough words for the young King Saul in the Old Testament for not ruling as a king should. In fact, Saul was failing not only as a king, but also as a man. The prophet scowled at him, "Though you are little in your own eyes, are you not the head of the tribes of Israel? The LORD anointed you king over Israel. And the LORD sent you on a mission" (1 Sam.

15:17–18). In other words, "The Lord has anointed you king; now act like a king!" Can you imagine if we talked in such a manner to a young man coming out of high school? Would he not crumble and cower before his accuser? What happened? Why are boys and young men unable to be men, let alone reach their true potential?

Boys were once raised in the shadow of their fathers and grandfathers, and mentoring happened as a natural result of interaction with other men. Sure, it was not gentle and tolerant, but a father knew that his son would one day leave his side and that he needed to prepare his son to encounter the world with maturity and self-confidence. Today, boys are left to be guided by strangers with competing agendas or to government committees who are pursuing alternative goals. They seek to re-create men to be domesticated or nonthreatening and to conform them to a sterile, reordered world.

I once met with an editor to discuss the prospect of writing a book about mentoring, and the issue of feminism surfaced. I maintained that the current condition of men could not be considered without weighing both the positive and negative influence of feminism on our families and our culture. He would have none of it and snapped back, "That is like Adam blaming Eve for the fall of man in the garden." Well, that is a charming, well-rehearsed response, but it also shows ignorance of the truth.

For too many years now, the feminist movement (as well as the homosexual lobby) has been above criticism. Attempts to give healthy, helpful, constructive criticism to these movements have been met with anger and resistance. Legitimate movements can withstand criticism and grow through open discourse. History will record the good of the feminist movement but will not hide its destructive influence.

In fact, I believe that feminism is not so much about equality as it is about power. And this is the core of the problem: would anyone argue against the fact that young men are naturally destined to brandish power? This power was intended to embolden a father, a soldier, a leader, or a productive member of the community. Nevertheless, social engineers have done everything in their power to destroy the possibility that, one day, a young man will assume his position among us and wield this power, even if it is for the good of us all. This will not be easy to accept and will even infuriate some. But for the sake of our families and communities, this must be considered.

Few boys today have had a male teacher (other than a coach) before graduating from high school. Boys are never given reading material that speaks to their hearts (such as a biography of a great man or a book on a battle or the frontier). Young men are given an enormous dose of feminist theory in our universities and colleges, and the schools themselves have been subjected to Title IX of the Equity in Education Act. And consider these points:

• There are approximately forty-seven active women's colleges in the United States, while, as of December 2008, there were only three nonreligious institutions in the United States that were recognized as four-year men's colleges (Hampden-Sydney College, Virginia; Morehouse College, Georgia; and Wabash College, Indiana).
• "According to the United States Department of Education, the average eleventh-grade American boy now writes at the same level as the average eighth-grade girl."[18]

---

[18] National Center for Education Statistics, *Trends in Education Equity for Girls and Women* (Washington, D.C.: U.S. Government Printing Office, 2004), 18.

- Money "poured in" to raise girls' math and science scores to boys' levels, but not to raise boys' lower reading scores.[19]
- From 1985 to 1997, more than 21,000 collegiate positions for male athletes disappeared. More than 359 teams for men have vanished since 1992. Christine Stolba of the Independent Women's Forum commented that between 1993 and 1999 alone, the Title IX commission eliminated "53 men's golf teams, 39 men's track teams, 43 wrestling teams, and 16 baseball teams." In addition, she reported, "the University of Miami's diving team, which has produced 15 Olympic athletes, is gone."[20]

More specifically, social engineers have prevented boys from being properly mentored, discouraging them from congregating and removing any semblance of male initiation. Much would be corrected if men were allowed these three essential fundamentals to form a proper and dependable male infrastructure.

In 1995, I was assigned to a medium-size parish of mixed blue- and white-collar families in the center of our diocese. One Sunday morning outside the church, I found myself before a tribunal of three teenage boys who were intent on interrogating me on my spirituality, my theology, and my philosophy of life. Some of their questions were incredibly challenging; some were accompanied by nervous laughter; and some were personally revelatory. The young men even coached me and suggested which of my answers needed work or more clarity!

---

[19] Hymowitz, *Manning Up*, 73.
[20] Steven E. Rhoads, *Taking Sex Differences Seriously* (San Francisco: Encounter Books, 2004), 161.

Three hours later, we were still at it, and they showed little interest in bringing the inquisition to a close. These three young men pressed me to make such encounters available to their male peers. It was from that encounter that the idea of forming a fraternity for young men of the parish was conceived. The result was a group of high school boys interested in faith, fraternity, service, and self-development. Based on the structure of the Knights Templar, governance was directed by the master (the master of the order), the seneschal (the second in command to the master), the marshal (the master of ceremonies, especially for liturgies), the commander (responsible for social events, service projects, and so forth), the draper (equivalent to a treasurer), brother knights, and confrères (adult male mentors). The young men were given authority over the Order, as it is called, with the hope that leadership skills would develop.

Their formation, intentionally informal, included camping trips in the Blue Ridge Mountains, leadership training, peer accountability, prayer and religious formation, and mentoring. An initiation rite was developed in which candidates were "knighted" and welcomed into the brotherhood. Outside observers might mock the initiation rite as trite or puerile, but the young men always approached initiation with sincere reverence and seriousness. The young men were held to the following honor code, which is as old as the Order and enforced by the brothers:

1. In all things, we are aware of God: our place in His plan, our need of His grace, and always conscious of all we have received from Him. A good man willingly submits to God's wisdom, not His own.
2. To sustain our ability to fight the spiritual battle, we frequent the sacrament of Holy Communion and the

sacrament of Reconciliation as often as possible. These sacraments are to be seen as the source of our strength.

3. As we are defenders of God's Holy Church, we accept our responsibility of learning the truth she teaches and are not afraid, reluctant, or even hesitant to defend her honor.

4. As men, we never underestimate the power of our witness to the truth of Jesus Christ and His Church. Hence, we conduct ourselves as Catholic gentlemen at all times, by purity of action, decency in speech, modesty in dress, respect toward others, and a good-natured spirit.

When a member failed to keep the honor code, he was given a warning; if he refused to correct his behavior, he was dismissed from the brotherhood. In addition, the young men were encouraged to abide by the principles in the document "See You on the Other Side" (see the appendix). The men were pressed never to "underestimate the power they have as young men to witness to Jesus Christ," and they took that precept seriously.

The success of the effort can be ascertained in the growth witnessed in the lives of its members. Not all were profoundly impacted, but the ideology of the fraternity could change the life of anyone who embraced the Order's ideals. The young men were given a purpose and a place to belong, were treated with respect, and were challenged to live up to a higher standard. Only young men with potential were admitted. If a man had something to give or had potential, he was welcomed; if he was not able to give or was indifferent to his potential, he was not extended an invitation.

From the beginning, the change in the young men was evident in the focus, purpose, maturity, and ever-growing selflessness they showed. It was not uncommon to see a member mentoring a younger brother, or a confrère relating life experiences to a group of brothers, or a cadre of brothers correcting a wayward brother in the ways of the honor code. The young men's witness affected the parish as well: liturgies became more solemn and exciting; prayers more fervent and purposeful.

Even the most ardent opponents of the Order began to see the benefits of the young men's work, and many become great supporters. This is not to mention young women, who are intensely attracted to mature young men with a purpose.

Nobody can deny the Order's success or its importance in the life of a young man. Take Thomas, for example. The last time he saw his biological father was through the back window of his mother's car as she drove away. He was only four years old. Thomas's father was an alcoholic and a drug addict and could not be trusted with his son. Even though Thomas had the support of a kind stepfather, by high school he had settled for complacency and mediocrity. He was tall, athletic, quiet, and, it could be said, at risk. During his sophomore year, he was introduced to the Knights. Thomas is now serving his country in the navy. He is a loving husband and delights in his young son. He prays, reads, volunteers, studies, and is frequently sought out by his fellow sailors for advice and counsel. He is a good man. Thomas attributes much of who he is to his involvement with the Knights and readily admits that, through the Order, he was able to avoid drugs, alcohol, illicit sex, and other negative influences. Perhaps none of this seems noteworthy or spectacular or even worth mentioning, but it means everything in the world to Thomas's son.

Three essential fundamentals — mentoring, fraternity, and initiation — change a man and change the world. Or, as Frederick

Douglass asserted: "It is better to build strong sons than to repair broken men."

Mentoring

Before we consider the consequences of the absence of mentoring, let us first consider egalitarianism—which should be rather easy, as it is all around us. Egalitarianism includes the natural heresy of the genderless person. The idea that there are no differences between the sexes would be laughable if so many people had not accepted the notion. Please take note: you cannot raise a boy as you would a girl and expect to have good results (and vice versa). Here, I could cite several enlightening but ignored opinions and studies,[21] but that seems pointless.

Let us try logic. That cute little boy whom we dress in gender-neutral clothing, force to play games that prohibit competition, punish when he exhibits aggression, and teach in the same manner we instruct girls will one day experience stunning growth and physical prowess. How will he use that prowess? Long ago, boys were trained, mentored, and prepared for the day they would "come into their own," and, for the most part, they were ready. Guided by the virtues, they would wield their natural power justly.

---

[21] Richard Fitzgibbons and Joseph Nicolosi, "When Boys Won't Be Boys: Childhood Gender Identity Disorder," *Lay Witness* (June 2001), posted at Catholic Education Resource Center, https://www.catholiceducation.org/en/marriage-and-family/sexuality/when-boys-won-t-be-boys-childhood-gender-indentity-disorder.html; Hoff Sommers, *The War Against Boys*; Sean Kullman, "Invitation to a Dialogue: Helping Boys Succeed" (letter to the editor), *New York Times*, February 23, 2015; Kenneth Zucker and Susan Bradley, *Gender Identity Disorder and Psychosexual Problems in Children and Adolescents* (New York: Guilford, 1995).

The way today's boys are raised can be compared to a family raising a lion cub. Sure, the cub is cuddly and cute. It lounges in the family room and eats a lot of food. It plays its curious games and rambles about the house. But what happens when that cub matures physically and discovers its power? If it has not been trained and prepared, it will likely eat someone. A similar neglect in raising boys results in bullying, domestic abuse, gang violence, and domestic terror.

In the Middle Ages, town and country were terrorized by gangs of young men who were reckless and abusive, and society could do little to correct their cruel behavior. But Holy Mother Church intervened. Recognizing—and even appreciating—the natural power and strength of these young men, the Church asked them to place their might at the service of the good. These young men were asked to make solemn vows to protect widows and orphans and to defend the Church as a band of brothers. Hence, Europe witnessed the birth of chivalry and the appearance of the medieval knight.[22]

I was astounded by the negative reaction I got when I announced that I was starting the Knights of St. John for high school boys. Yet the fraternity was hugely successful, especially for the growth of the members (not to mention the faith and vibrancy of the parish). Many of the young men were amazed that someone would take an interest in helping them become better men. Lives were changed. Even so, time after time, I would hear, "And what are you doing for the girls?" and "You are teaching these boys to feel superior and arrogant." I would respond with politeness, but interiorly I was annoyed. Nearly everyone admits

---

[22] Brad Miner, *The Compleat Gentleman: The Modern Man's Guide to Chivalry* (Dallas: Spence Publishing, 2004), 20.

(finally) that girls have enjoyed much more success than boys, since a disproportionate share of our educational and professional efforts are reserved for girls. Social feminist Christina Hoff Sommers has masterfully proven this.[23] As incomprehensible as it may seem, social engineers simply do not want boys to be mentored.

Many fathers, whose most important work included mentoring their sons and teaching them to become men, are commonly absent. A study by Carl Auerbach and Louise Silverstein concluded, "We do not believe that the data support the conclusion that fathers are essential to child well-being,"[24] even though the authors admitted plainly that it is preferable for fathers to be involved in the lives of their children. Their conclusion is grossly unfair to children and incomprehensible to rational adults. In 2015, Great Britain was shocked to learn that "a father" made children's top-ten most requested Christmas gifts. The mentor-disciple relationship has been broken, and too many men are not around to teach boys how to brandish their natural power and develop their character.

Forbidding Men to Congregate

In my experience in forming men, I have discovered that one of the most significant sources for positive growth in men is fraternity. By "fraternity," I mean any and all opportunities for men to come together for constructive purposes: building, hunting, traveling, discovering, working, defending, farming, or worshipping.

---

[23] *The War Against Boys*; "School Has Become Too Hostile to Boys," *Time*, August 19, 2013, http://ideas.time.com/2013/08/19/school-has-become-too-hostile-to-boys/.

[24] Carl F. Auerbach and Louise B. Silverstein, "Deconstructing the Essential Father," *American Psychologist* 54, no. 6 (1999): 397–407.

Purpose is necessary; men do not come together to "share" or "relate" to one another, as women do. When men congregate, they are transformed in a powerful manner by competition, camaraderie, the accomplishment of challenging goals, the defense of the country, and the overcoming of great odds. A man cannot know himself, his abilities, his limitations, his power, or even his tenderness if he is not transformed in a group of trusted men. The lack of these opportunities is causing a crisis in our country.

Consider the many opportunities for constructive camaraderie that have been denied to men. Men are almost forbidden to congregate in our contemporary world. There are no gentlemen's clubs (nonsexual) or civic clubs where men can smoke a cigar, read the paper, and talk about politics, community, sports, or family and be mentored by older men in the club. Women are now encouraged to enter motorcycle clubs, go on hunting trips, join male sports teams, and be involved in other traditionally male interests and pursuits. Why? Is it because women have suddenly developed interests in these pursuits? Perhaps most grievous of all, women are now permitted in combat. Defense of one's country has always been a "sacred" vocation for men — in which they pledged themselves to each other in a fraternal bond. Although many would like to argue the point, there is no reason whatsoever for a woman to be in combat. Yet new combat regulations have removed another place for male growth, purpose, and even identity. Have you ever wondered why so many in secular society revile the Catholic Church with vicious hatred and gross intolerance? Could it be the all-male priesthood?

For years, the men who run in my circle have enjoyed "guy time." What is notable is the willingness of wives and girlfriends to permit and make space for such gatherings, retreats, and trips. These women intuitively know the value of such activity for men, and they know that, when their men return, they will be better men, husbands, and fathers. Of course, we do not consider destructive or immoral behavior to be a part of productive "guy time." Men must be intentional about their time together as men.

Initiation

The problem caused by the absence of an initiation rite is profound. When a young man has reached maturity, how does he know he is truly a good and worthy man? By what standard is he measured? Who is the gatekeeper who can judge the boy "successful" and grant him entrance to the world of men? Who will watch to see if the young man is using his power for positive and constructive purposes? Absent that rite of passage whereby a boy comes to know he is a man and, simultaneously, that he has an enormous responsibility to God, family, and country, his development will be stunted. He may be a man physically, but emotionally, he is still a boy—a very worrisome combination.

I think many would be surprised by the desire of young men, when they are made aware of these ancient initiation rites, to earn the right to be initiated into the male community. Yet, here again, attempts to initiate high school or college-age men are met with resistance. On the surface, a mentor may be accused of dark activity, inappropriateness, or even oppression. Even though the rite of initiation is rarely understood, it is almost universally condemned.

3

THE BENEFITS OF FORMING MEN

As John F. Kennedy said, "When the tide comes in, all the boats rise." If women are to continue their laudable advancement in our communities, it cannot be at the expense of men, and vice versa. To build a just and harmonious society, men and women both must come to realize their full potential.

Ironically, it is women themselves who are raising concerns about the stagnated, ill-developed men in our culture. Women have published books urging men to "man up." Many young women cannot find mature, well-rounded men they might wish to marry.

In his book *Boys Adrift*, Dr. Leonard Sax related correspondence he received from a frustrated woman unable to find a mate of equal stature. She wrote, "Last year, after more bad dates than I can count, I gave up. I got myself a nice 25-year-old boy toy, whom I can call when I want and ignore when I want. He's not that bright, but who cares? There's no future. He lives at home with his parents."[25] The situation this woman describes is

---

[25] Leonard Sax, M.D., Ph.D., *Boys Adrift: The Five Factors Driving the Growing Epidemic of Unmotivated Boys and Underachieving Young Men* (New York: Basic Books, 2007), 138.

certainly not good for women, and it is a horrendous description of the condition we find young men in today.

It has been amply documented by Christina Hoff Sommers, for example, that boys who are taught almost exclusively by women in our schools are rarely afforded the developmental exercises and lessons that boys need to become well-adjusted men.[26] As innocuous as this might sound, it is catastrophic. In some cases, women are well aware of the needs of boys, but to reiterate, in most cases today, advancing the cause of boys is perceived as a threat to the success of girls.

Be assured, my efforts here have an equal and just society as the ultimate goal. A society in which boys are intentionally neglected and men are at a disadvantage or are restricted in their natural rights by the legislative or judicial system will not benefit anyone. Eventually, men and women must reject the idea that has emerged in recent decades: that men and women are in some way competitors and not, as nature would have it, complementary. Nature will not allow one gender to be neutralized or eliminated. It will require the success of both genders if we are to live in a productive, fruitful society to the benefit of all.

Over the past few decades, girls seem to have been indoctrinated with the error that they cannot be successful, both personally and professionally, unless they accomplish tasks and vocations traditionally fulfilled by boys and men. Ironically, this is feminist misogyny. The unspoken thought of such feminism is the notion that women must be engaged in masculine pursuits in order to realize equality. Anyone who asserts publicly that

---

[26] Hoff Sommers, *The War Against Boys.*

women have a natural instinct and gift to nurture children is accused of manipulating women to make them believe they are somehow doomed to an allegedly menial, unfulfilling vo-cation — as if raising and nurturing children, which, in most societies throughout history, was held as the most essential and important activity of both men and women, one that ensures the very future of entire communities, is somehow trivial or unim-portant! Hopefully, someday very soon, we will begin to see that the most important pursuit of any community is the nurturing, rearing, and mentoring of young people. If such activity were held in proper regard, everything as we know it today would improve: the role of women and men in the lives of children would change drastically, reflecting the wisdom of thousands of generations before us.

We would do well to acknowledge that many women through-out the world are, in fact, horribly oppressed and mistreated by the men in their lives. This is seen especially in third-world countries and communities rooted in archaic or fundamentalist religious tendencies, but it can be seen even in advanced democratic countries. The 2017 exposition of countless sex offenses at the hands of men is evidence of this problem. This is unacceptable and must be rooted out of our communities, our thinking, and our way of life.

Many of us, however, believe that the most effective way to assist women and prevent their mistreatment and oppression is the proper rearing and formation of young men.

During the 2014 Global Summit of Women, the topic of abuse and violence against women was addressed. Not surprisingly, men were not invited to the discussion. Men are taught and held accountable by other men, a fact that the organizers effectively ignored. The surest way to keep women safe is to tutor boys and young men not in sensitivity training but in the virtues. This cannot be easily dismissed.

Mistreatment of women is simply unacceptable.

Also unacceptable is the subtle movement (especially in so-called advanced countries) that has worked to suppress young men in a sort of collective revenge or, worse, considers the oppression of men a way to bring about a balance of power.

For the present, it would be best to allow those who hold rigidly to these ideologies to go their own way and leave us to the work that we must do for the young men for whom we are responsible. In addition, perhaps society might reach a happy medium whereby, if people are not concerned with the development and happiness of both genders, they would at least refrain from suppressing one or the other.

I have traveled to many places to deliver what I consider an important message about the current situation of men. Many times, perhaps most of the time, the men whom I addressed reacted with hostility and anger about what I said. I tried various ways of presenting my data and my conclusions but never received a more positive response. Finally, I realized that the cause of the anger was not my style or my delivery; it my message: it was purely countercultural.

I was working to draw attention to the unrealized potential and the serious failure of many men in our communities. I was also offering analysis and criticism of current schools of thought that hold egalitarianism, fairness, tolerance, and "niceness" as the alternatives to time-tested virtues. To my amazement, I found that many men — having been reared in a culture that has blamed the heterosexual male for all its troubles and difficulties — found my words "overly simplistic," "offensive," "antiquated," and oppressive toward women. Ironically, in most of these cases, I was not even talking about women.

Patriarchal Society

For many years, young men and women in our colleges and universities have been given a healthy dose of skepticism about ancient cultures and civilizations and their impact on modern society. While sitting on a religious panel at a state university, I was asked to explain the Church's rationale for an all-male priesthood. When I concluded my remarks, a woman on the panel who served as a minister in a Christian church, turned and nearly yelled, "Patriarchy!" and pointed an accusing finger at me. Her loathing for our patriarchal history was on display.

"Patriarchy" today is largely described in subjective terms. *Everyday Feminism* defines it as "a sociopolitical and cultural system that values masculinity over femininity"; in other words, patriarchy is simply an oppressive social construct that naturally favors men and oppresses women. Some consider the world—dominated by men—to be the result of intentional social design and not at all the result of circumstance. In such a design, patriarchy seeks to prevent women from attaining success as it provides the justification needed to degrade women in general. In such a system that deliberately favors men, women would have to be taught to fight if they wished to garner respect and enjoy economic and cultural advances.

I do not claim to be an anthropologist, but I believe we owe a debt of gratitude to the patriarchs of the ancient and more contemporary world. No doubt, injustices occurred; but the fact that humans even exist and have thrived on the planet as long as they have is a tribute to both patriarchy and matriarchy. In a lecture, Dr. John Bergsma, a professor of theology at Franciscan University of Steubenville, noted that "most cemeteries in antiquity consist mostly of women because men are far, far more likely to die at sea, die in battle, die while traveling, etc., and thus not be buried in a traditional cemetery. Cemeteries in antiquity tend to be 60 percent or more female."[27] Men died defending their homeland, hunting and gathering, opening trade routes, securing resources, and so forth. It is hard to imagine a patriarchal world in which men had time or energy to oppress women. Patriarchy was about survival for everyone.

Granted, ancient texts often describe women as inferior or in the possession of men who ruled them and restricted their freedom. Indeed, social reconstructionists even glean Scripture passages that make women seem oppressed and prevented from enjoying the same rights and privileges as men. A common example is St. Paul's unpopular instruction: "Wives, be subject to your husbands, as to the Lord. For the husband is the head of the wife as Christ is the head of the Church, his body, and is himself its Savior" (Eph. 5:22–23).

How should we understand this passage? Is St. Paul misogynistic in his outlook, attempting to suppress women and negate the contribution they can make to our communities and Church?

No. St. Paul, composing his letters in the first century, was reflecting the communal structure and societal customs of his time. With complete empathy for women, he witnessed the seemingly deferential role they played within the family. The vocation of a mother and wife, he observed, was characterized by self-sacrificing love and life-giving nurturing.

Thus, St. Paul encouraged women, in the heroic sacrifices required of them, to embrace their service to husband and family as if they were at the service of Christ Jesus Himself, thus winning graces for their own sanctity and the good of their families.

---

[27] John Bergsma, *The Dead Sea Scrolls and the Jewish Roots of the Church*, 18 CDs (New Orleans, LA: Catholic Productions, n.d.).

He was not, in any way whatsoever, encouraging men to oppress women. As evidence, he later goes on to instruct another group of people: "Slaves, be obedient to those who are your earthly masters, with fear and trembling, in singleness of heart, as to Christ ... doing the will of God from the heart, rendering service with a good will as to the Lord and not to men, knowing that whatever good any one does, he will receive the same again from the Lord, whether he is a slave or free" (Eph. 6:5–8).

It would be foolish to insist, in a contemporary, self-justifying way, that St. Paul was somehow endorsing the enslavement of people. He lived in a world in which slavery was an acceptable manner of life, and many of his followers undoubtedly were members of this unfortunate class. He is really saying that if this is the situation in which a person finds himself, he should work as if serving Jesus Christ, who came to serve and not to be served, and model Christ in such a manner that he would surely be rewarded by the God who sees all. He is saying the same to women of his century and urging them to consider their service as service to Christ Himself.

There are many other examples: Christians are to submit to their pastors (see Heb. 13:17); men are to submit to those who govern them (Rom. 13:1–7; 1 Pet. 2:13–17); and everyone is to submit to God (James 4:7). Lucifer, of course, refused to submit to anyone, including God, and the result was devastating (see Isa. 14).

Finally, turning to men in these passages, St. Paul placed a burden upon them that most would consider even more ominous: "Husbands, love your wives, as Christ loved the Church and gave himself up for her, that he might sanctify her" (Eph. 5:25–26). Again, just as women are to entrust themselves in heroic selflessness to men and their children, so, too, men must be ready to love and serve their wives and their families, even to the point of death—a challenging vocation.

As we seek to mentor young men, we must encourage them to look beyond themselves and place themselves, in imitation of Jesus Christ, at the service of those around them. "For as many of you as were baptized into Christ have put on Christ. There is neither Jew nor Greek, there is neither slave nor free, there is neither male nor female; for you are all one in Christ Jesus" (Gal. 3:27–28). The sheer power of a man is ordered to the protection and service of his wife, his family, his community, and his church.

Part 2

THE MENTOR

When I was a newly ordained priest, I found in George Weigel's *Witness to Hope: The Biography of Pope John Paul II* one of the most influential statements I had ever read about mentoring. Mr. Weigel interviewed a man who had participated in the Catholic youth organization of Father Karol Wojtyla (later Pope John Paul II). His name was Stanislaw Rybicki, and he shared this insight about his relationship with the future pope: "Today, many priests try to be like the kids. We were trying to be like him."[28]

This is essential for the mentor to bear in mind in order to be successful and be of great value to his disciple. "A disciple is not above his teacher," Jesus tells us, "but everyone when he is fully taught will be like his teacher" (Luke 6:40). Thus, it starts with the mentor. Long before he interacts with young people, he is obliged to look at himself and, perhaps even with the assistance of friends, assess his own character, maturity, reputation, and motivation. The mentor should be "powerful" enough to engage the imagination of his disciple, giving him a model (without excuses) that he can emulate in his own life.

---

[28] George Weigel, *Witness to Hope: The Biography of Pope John Paul II* (New York: HarperCollins, 1999), 105.

We are not talking about perfection. What you will accomplish as a mentor will be taught via your actions, your manner of conduct, the level of your maturity, and your ability to apply creative solutions, maintain an even temper, and care about others. Concretely, this means that when you are with your disciple, you will not laugh at inappropriate jokes, attend inappropriate movies, expose minors to alcohol or older fellows to drunkenness, use foul language or take the name of the Lord in vain, violate boundaries, mock or ridicule the young man, and so forth. I will say more about this later, but the point is this: in the midst of the confusion of our dark culture, broken relationships, and malaise, your disciple needs a model more than anything else; and you may very well have been called to provide that model for him.

Anyone who is active in sports is familiar with the adage "The best coaches were not the best players." What a consolation to a mentor! The success of a mentor has nothing to do with his personal perfection or impeccability. As a matter of fact, a good and worthy mentor is rarely without faults, weaknesses, or failures, for it is because of his own faults, weaknesses, and failures that he is able to empathize, understand, and strategize. It is often said that only a recovering alcoholic can assist an alcoholic, for a recovering alcoholic has the capacity to detect the truth and has the wherewithal to understand the difficult situation in which an alcoholic might find himself. With such insight and experience, he knows how best to coach and encourage another alcoholic who may find himself in a desperate or even a hopeless situation. In the same way, a man who has lived, tried, and failed, faced fears, overcome challenges (not always on the first attempt), and remains on the field ready to fight can understand the difficult journey placed before a young man.

You must also resist the temptation to discount your ability as a mentor. It is ingrained in the psyche of a boy or a young man to please his father or his father figure. If you can give in an unselfish, disinterested way, you have all that is necessary to mentor a son or a grandson, a neighbor or a student, a fellow parishioner or a boy at risk. Society has convinced us that "older men" are irrelevant. If you believe such nonsense, you have lost the capacity to mentor. If you believe in yourself, however — if you believe you have something to give; if you can observe, reason, and reach conclusions — you can mentor and will have much to offer. I can tell you with all certainty that boys and young men understand this. If you approach a young man for his own sake with only his welfare in mind, you have what it takes to be a mentor.

Every boy or young man deserves to have in his life at least one man who has verbally or nonverbally committed himself to his welfare and has selflessly pledged himself to his disciple's future. It is that important. A mentor accompanies, teaches, challenges, pushes, disciplines, consoles, encourages, and celebrates his disciple. A mentor is a hero in the sense that he is never far from the disciple and is immensely important in the disciple's life, but is nearly always unseen or in the background.

A mentor loves selflessly and anticipates the hour when his disciple will stand opposite him, look him in the face, thank him, turn, and depart. At that point, who knows where God might lead him? A true mentor loathes that day, but for the sake of his apprentice, he works tirelessly to ensure that it will happen; and, when it does, he knows that his joy and reward is the news he receives from time to time of his disciple's success.

4

THE LIFE THE MENTOR CAN GIVE HIS DISCIPLE AND THE FEAR OF MENTORING

The most important mentor in the life of a boy or a young man is his father. In a perfect world, a father would raise his sons carefully and intentionally while relying on the assistance provided by a community of good, worthy, hardworking men. When a boy or a young man lacks this environment or has no father (other than through natural causes, such as death), the deficiencies are readily apparent. This has been contested over the years, but more and more, those voices are going silent in light of the evidence that is now glaring all around us.

Absent the father or the male mentor, research and even observable experience show that boys and young men are susceptible to a vast number of male-specific developmental issues.[29] These include the following:

---

[29] Guy Corneau, *Absent Fathers, Lost Sons: The Search for Masculine Identity* (Boston: Shambhala, 1991), 20; Steven E. Rhoades, *Taking Sex Differences Seriously* (San Francisco: Encounter Books, 2004), 79; Kay S. Hymowitz, "Where Have the Good Men Gone?", *Wall Street Journal*, February 19, 2011, posted at Catholic Education Resource Center, http://www.catholiceducation.org/en/controversy/marriage/where-have-the-good-men-gone.

- Absent a male role model, especially a father, a young man's psychosexual life will not be ordered to his or anyone else's good. His emotional life will be underdeveloped. He will experience a "validation deficit" that will make him vulnerable to pornography, masturbation, promiscuity, cohabitation, and a less stable marriage. Human sexual activity will not be the means by which he gives deeply of himself in a union with his spouse, but a frustrated attempt to answer the age-old question, "Is it good that I exist?" He will not be equipped to understand the meaning and goodness of self-giving, nor will he understand the sacred purpose of sexual union.
- A boy whose emotional life has been neglected by his father is more likely to struggle with homosexuality or, at the very least, be confused about his sexual identity. On the other side of that coin, boys who are used or inappropriately manipulated by their mothers and neglected by their fathers are more likely to struggle with narcissism.

---

html; Gerard van den Aardweg, "On the Psychogenesis of Homosexuality," *Linacre Quarterly* 78, no. 3 (2011): 330–354; Hoff Sommers, *The War Against Boys*; Carolyn Moynihan, "Father's Day: The Difference a Dad Makes," Mercatornet, June 19, 2015, https://www.mercatornet.com/family_edge/view/fathers-day-the-difference-a-dad-makes/16378; Sally C. Curtin, Margaret Warner, and Holly Hedegaard, *Suicide Rates for Females and Males by Race and Ethnicity: United States, 1999 and 2014* (Washington, D.C.: National Center for Health Statistics, 2016), https://www.cdc.gov/nchs/data/hestat/suicide/rates_1999_2014.pdf; Kat Eschner, "Three New Things Science Says about Dads," Smithsonian.com, June 16, 2017, http://www.smithsonianmag.com/smart-news/three-new-things-science-says-about-dads-180963698/.

Both are certainly debilitating to a young man, and, as a result, he will suffer greatly in self-condemnation.

• Lacking a male role model who selflessly loves him, respects him, and teaches him, a young man very well may display feminine mannerisms or characteristics. Of course, the word "feminine" is a very poor descriptor, as a beautiful and strong woman once lamented to me — and she is correct. What is typically meant by "effeminacy" is a male softness, an absence of rigor, a laxity, a lack of interest in traditionally male pursuits, or a showy buffoonery (trying to act like a woman). Thus, this is not truly feminine behavior; it is more accurately effeminacy and is more akin to boyish behavior displayed by men who have passed beyond the adolescent stage. Even men who are considered to be characteristically masculine, such as athletes, can sometimes display subtle effeminate characteristics.

• Without a mature man who can listen and assist a boy in negotiating the difficulties of life, a boy will tend to think in circles, unable to comprehend or understand major life events, such as death or failure. This results in scrupulosity or obsessive or compulsive thinking or behaving.

• Men who have not been mentored are usually emotionally deprived and have a poor sense of self-worth and, as is to be expected, nearly always lack self-confidence.

As tragic as this might seem, the greater tragedy is that *all of this* can easily be avoided. But before it can be avoided, it must be understood.

I am often asked to talk with students in many settings. Once, before I entered a freshman classroom, the religion teacher turned and stood between her classroom door and me. She looked apprehensive, her posture was stiff, and her face exhibited chronic fatigue. Something in the class was causing her anxiety and frustration. She leaned forward and lowered her voice, "Father, I need to warn you about Oliver. He has been my challenge this year." The frustration was clearly visible; she did not attempt to hide a mixture of anger, fear, and hopelessness. "I think he may have ADHD or a mild case of Asperger's syndrome. His parents are divorced, he is utterly defiant, and he ceaselessly disrupts the class." I smiled to reassure her and, with confidence, told her, "He will not be a problem."

While I presented to the class, the teacher sat vigilantly at her desk, awaiting the inevitable disruption. When I completed my lesson, I opened the floor for clarifications, questions, and debate. As if on cue, Oliver's hand shot into the air, and he flashed an impish grin. Not surprisingly, the entire class seemed to groan, which only confirmed their teacher's frustration. Oliver was thrilled. He was on stage again, and he asked the most ridiculous question he could imagine. He had played this game before and was eager to begin the exchange. But today would be different.

I squared off before him and looked him in the eye and did something that may not have happened to him for a long time: I took him seriously. I praised him for his question and took his thought even deeper. Soon, we were having a discussion, as if the two of us were alone in the room. He worked hard not to allow his interest in the subject to be seen by his classmates. The conversation was insightful and enriching for both of us.

There was no magic. I am but an ordinary man. Some would see in Oliver only an incorrigible boy who is prone to outbursts, laziness, and disregard, but I saw a young man with potential, and I treated him as such. Potential, from the Latin noun *potentia* — force, power, might, ability, and capacity — was buried beneath the surface of his false exterior, an exterior he had managed for survival. He was coming into his own; his entire being communicated a reserve of strength and untapped ability. Emotionally, perhaps, he was behind the game, but here was a man trying desperately to emerge from the boy. He needed only what most of his male peers need today: to be mentored.

It is unjust to ignore or disparage the power a man must use to lift a young man or boy from darkness, confusion, and despair; we cannot allow that to happen. This is so important that even young men instinctively know this to be true. On several occasions, young men have come to my office and have boldly said, "Teach me, Father" or "Show me what I must do" or "Tell me what to read" or "Give me a challenge." Like the boy in the story above, dramatic change can occur in a young man. It is true that, at times, this change will occur only after long, very difficult work, but transformation is certainly possible.

Man, depending on how you define the term, has lived and died on Earth for more than four hundred thousand years. To do so well, he has developed an organic system, a thoroughly dependable, yet unwritten, set of rules that guided and informed older, more experienced generations in the mentoring and nurturing of the younger.

Today, masculine character seems to be powerless before extensive selfishness, a lack of male confidence, and an inability to mentor, but the primal instinct remains in man.

Mentoring is a relational pursuit. Mentoring has never been about groups; it concerns individuals: the interaction of father and son, grandfather and grandson, brother and brother, priest and disciple, teacher and student. One need not receive diplomas or training to mentor. In many cases, it is a matter of empathy, asking oneself, "What did I need in the way of mentoring when I was this young man's age?" and responding to those instincts.

If you do not believe the situation is urgent, if you do not see the pressing need, put this book down and do not trouble yourself; it will be useless to you. But if you believe enough in the goodness of the young man near you and believe enough in yourself—if you believe that you have something important to offer him, even if in but a small way—please consider thoughtfully what is written here. Everyone should keep in mind—and I know this from experience—that there is preserved within the young man, perhaps miraculously, a yearning for virtue, goodness, honor, and self-sacrificing heroism. Once we identified and worried about children who were "at risk." Today, with a few exceptions, all children are at risk. Perhaps children, especially our sons, have been shoved aside by our concerns with technology, our material wealth, and our personal pursuits.

All of this notwithstanding, the life a man can give his disciple is without price. Simply showing a young man that you believe in him, recognize his true potential, and are willing to invest in him can rescue him from absurdity, mediocrity, and failure. And the reward for such work is tremendous.

Sitting at my desk one day, I received an e-mail from a young man I had not seen in over a year and will probably never see again. I was utterly and completely humbled by it. He said, in part, "I want to take a moment to express how grateful I am for all you have done for me in my formation as a man. Your mentorship has been an indispensable element in my education and formation. Thank you for the time and attention you gave me. I have grown immensely and overcome many fears under your guidance. Thanks for everything."

5

INDISPENSABLE CHARACTERISTICS
OF A MENTOR

By way of review, before the mentor engages a disciple, he must examine himself to determine whether he can accomplish the task of mentoring. A mentor need not be perfect, but he must be morally upstanding, respectable, and mature. Before mentoring, he may be required to pray and go to church; exercise and lose a few pounds; be more fully present to his family; and correct any glaring faults. A mentor must be able to model what a good and holy man is. A disciple will be motivated not so much by what is said to him, but by the actions and the character of the mentor. Only when a man is respected and admired will he be powerful enough to correct, challenge, and affirm. If not, he should seriously reconsider mentoring until he has gained credibility.

If a disciple respects you appropriately, he will even harbor a sense of reverential fear toward you. This does not mean fear of physical harm or abuse. I respect and admire my own mentor, a priest, so much that I fear him. When I visit his rectory, I nearly always have a good amount of anxiety before I arrive, even as I am excited to see him. It is because of this great respect I have for him that I receive everything he tells me with a profound and weighty consideration. If he were to tell me, and I hope he would not, that I am a fraud or a failure, I would take that judgment to be all but conclusive. Because of that, when he does affirm me — and this he does frequently — I receive it as irrefutable.

None of this is meant to discourage a mentor from engaging a young person. Mentoring is a profoundly sacred duty, and it is a singular privilege to be a part of a young person's life. Young people deserve the opportunity to be mentored and elevated. This should never be taken lightly. Do not underestimate the impact you can have on a young person. As has been detailed above, young people are at risk and nearly always see being mentored as a "rare privilege" or even as a "last chance."

Important characteristics required for good mentoring are disinterest, respect, honesty, authenticity and integrity, forthrightness, commitment, availability, vulnerability, and awareness of your limitations.

Disinterest

Disinterest is essential to good mentoring. Disinterest does not mean not interested in or not caring toward an individual. On the contrary, it means quite the opposite: your care and energy are completely and freely given to the disciple, and you seek absolutely nothing in return. If you do, in some way, benefit from the relationship, no foul. But you must never seek to gain personal benefit from the relationship.

A coach once told me that he demanded discipline and hard work from his team. He was not for wasting time or associating with a group of "losers," after all, and he told his players that he enjoyed winning and that he wanted to "get something out of this, too." There are two problems with the coach's attitude: first, he was coaching sixth graders and, second, he was using these young people for his own gratification or satisfaction. This is not acceptable. In any situation, adults should never use young people for their own benefit.

I was nearly run out of town once when addressing a group of youth ministers. Youth ministers are generally amazing people who care deeply about the welfare and growth of the young people given to their charge. Nonetheless, at this venue, I was trying to address the concept of "disinterest," urging my listeners to consider that in a mentoring situation, it is never about the mentor. The relationship is a sacred one whereby the mentor selflessly gives of himself, expecting nothing in return. Young people can be powerful in their youthfulness, and it is tempting to manipulate them in order that they might "like me" or "affirm me" or somehow "make me feel important or fulfilled." Taken to a radical degree, this can become grievously serious.

In this case, the group resisted my message. One man argued considerably, trying to justify the legitimacy of his own needs, and stated, "I enjoy being hugged or loved by the youth of my parish." If I were his pastor, I would ask him to step down from his position. In an era of confusion and hurt, we must respect appropriate boundaries, even emotional ones.

There may be times when a disciple might reject your advice or counsel, and this calls for disinterest. Your disciple might make a choice that you know will lead to his harm or to his failure. Nonetheless, you stand by your disciple and allow him his freedom. And should he fail, you should prepare to offer counsel or advice to help him to learn from his mistake. To become angry or stubborn in the face of the independent nature of a young man will get you (and him) nowhere.

On the other hand, and contrary to what we are taught today, you should be ready and eager to give counsel, to make your disciple aware of right and wrong, good and evil, and always with the hope that he will choose the better way.

In addition, you must never—let me stress it—*never* take credit for the success of your disciple, even when he insists on sharing his glory with you. A very quick, definitive way to end a mentoring relationship is for the mentor to brag about his involvement in the success of his disciple.

It is natural to desire credit for the investment you have made in an individual. But the same individual will recoil if he senses that you are using him in some manner. For example, you might be tempted to say, "I was instrumental in helping David overcome his addiction to drugs." No, not really. It was David who fought that fight. It was David who made the sacrifices, endured the suffering, and earned the crown of victory. Yes, it was also David who trusted you, who held firm because you believed in him. Tell him of your respect, but take no credit for his success, just as a good father would. That done, he will eagerly return to you to be mentored further. Your silent satisfaction comes in seeing him enjoy his success. And that is a sweet and enduring satisfaction for you.

Disinterest is the most necessary as well as the most challenging characteristic of a mentor. Consider, for example, a scenario in which you engage a young man in a profound relationship of mentoring. The relationship may require an enormous investment on your part. You may have prayed endlessly that the young man will soon turn a corner, and he may be close!

But what if news comes that he has decided to abandon the relationship and pursue other goals with other people? His new goals may be positive or negative; they may help him or not help him; but as a disinterested mentor, you must room for freedom. You should never confront your disciple with "What about my investment?" or "What about my friendship?" or "What is left for me?" Be confident that seeds have been planted, and pray that they sprout in good time.

A man willing to mentor a young person must push his anxiety aside, while scrupulously monitoring himself and observing well-positioned boundaries. A constant guide for the mentor is this: "Is my involvement with this young person for me, or is it for the good and well-being of my disciple?" If he always interacts with the good of his disciple in mind, and that can be clearly seen by others, he should have little need to worry. If a relationship ever does become about the mentor and his needs, he is well advised, even warned, to terminate the relationship and find his own fulfillment and joy in friendship with men of his own age.

Respect

I am often astounded by the way adults treat young people — as if they were five to ten years younger than they are. Adults typically place unhelpful restrictions and childish rules on young men. I am a man who follows the letter of the law. I have high expectations for the boys or young men in my charge, but I also treat them as men.

As mentioned earlier, I have been involved with a high school boys' fraternity for many years. In my work with these young men, I have always treated them with respect, given them my confidence, and harbored the expectation that they will behave as gentlemen. I have never been disappointed with their behavior. One night, in the mountains of Pennsylvania, I was awakened by hushed voices outside our cabin. Evidently, one of the young men had smuggled a bottle of whiskey into his backpack and proudly produced the bootleg after the chaperones and I had retired for the night. Now his peers were confronting the young man. "You know we have an honor code, and you know this will get Father in trouble," I heard one of them whisper. Another reiterated firmly, "Pour it out." I fell asleep listening to the gurgling of whiskey being poured onto the ground.

I have often thrown the keys of my vehicle to a young man and asked him to drive. Interiorly, I am a wreck and anxious about the safety of my vehicle. On the other hand, I can read the result in the face of the young man. It is a moment of trust and true belief in his capability — a simple act of trust, but he swells with confidence and relishes the fact that I respect him enough to step aside and allow him to take command.

Most men know that if you treat a boy like a man, he will act like a man. And, on the contrary, if you treat a man like a boy, do not be surprised when he acts like a boy. Have a general and outspoken expectation that the boys for whom you are responsible are men, and frequently remind them that you expect them to be gentlemen, and they will seldom disappoint. On the other hand, attempts to manipulate their behavior or to control unsuitable behavior will communicate to them that you do not trust them, and their time with you will become a contest — a contest they will be determined to win.

Honesty

Young people will cling to you for your honesty. They are shrouded in confusion today. You should be reluctant to add to that confusion, as when, for example, trophies are given for nothing more than participation. As a mentor, you should praise only when it is earned and only when your disciple is worthy of praise. If he has not earned your admiration or your respect, it should not be given. Otherwise, when he truly has earned your praise, it will mean nothing to him. That is not to say that he must go for long periods without your encouragement, something he will always need. Young men appreciate candor and even bluntness. If you must correct or discipline, he is more than capable of receiving such, but it will be received only if he trusts you and has no reason to question your honesty in the matter.

Consider Simon Peter as an example. After Peter has spent countless hours with his Teacher, Jesus turns to him with a question and puts him to the test: "Who do you say that I am?"

It is Peter, over the din of the other disciples, who declares Jesus to be "the Christ, the Son of the living God." In response, Jesus praises Peter by asserting, "Blessed are you, Simon Bar-Jona! For flesh and blood has not revealed this to you, but my Father who is in heaven" (Matt. 16:15–17). One can imagine the satisfaction that Peter enjoyed in this moment. He was learning and was successful in his attempt to use what Jesus had taught him. Jesus acknowledged with great satisfaction the progress his disciple had made and even lifted Peter to a new level in their relationship. Jesus was eager to praise and lavished His approval without reservation.

Yet, not even a paragraph later, after Jesus has told His disciples about the suffering and death that await Him in Jerusalem, Peter attempts to rebuke Jesus by saying, "God forbid, Lord! This shall never happen to you." Jesus responds with candor and honesty and with His own rebuke for Peter: "Get behind me, Satan! You are a hindrance to me; for you are not on the side of God, but of men" (Matt. 16:22–23). Surely this stung Peter to his core. But it was honest. It was an assessment of the truth. Jesus knew Peter could handle the truth, even if reluctantly.

Likewise, when we are mentoring our own disciples, we should never fear adherence to the truth. It is beneficial to consider carefully how the truth should be delivered, but we should not question the approach used by Jesus.

The truth can be liberating and healing. Many times, I have listened to a young person tell me the story of his life. We all have wounds and hurts in our past, but few of us have the wherewithal to take account of our history and draw meaningful conclusions. Divorce can be one of those devastating and destructive forces in a person's life. Simply empathizing with a victim of divorce can be truly poignant. For example, you could say to a young man, "I am sorry. This should never have happened to you; it was not right. Children are not supposed to be raised in such circumstances." This might be painful for adults who have themselves experienced divorce firsthand, but it is liberating for a young person who has been told all his life that the divorce he experienced was somehow "normal." It is not. A divorced woman told me that her children were mature and had adapted to their new circumstances with ease. Meanwhile, both her son and daughter had been in my office sobbing at the thought of the demise of their family.

At times, a mentor must be truly and directly honest: "Your behavior is detrimental to your future," or "You are better than that," or "You are not living up to your true potential," or "You owe So-and-so an apology," or "You need to consider the consequences of your actions." I do not believe in the adage that you must accept a person "where he is," as it often becomes an excuse to remain static.

This is the work we are about: helping boys to become the men they are meant to be. Praise God, I have had men and women in my life who had the ability to hold me accountable and who appreciated me enough to tell me when I had to work harder or make changes. What good, by way of mentoring, would they have been to me otherwise? Again, many times we are afraid to tell a person the truth, even when it is with great compassion. Of course, how and when we tell a person the truth requires great tact and skill. But we must resist the temptation to withhold the truth. Perhaps there is a fear that our disciple will not appreciate us for what we tell him. Not so, typically; more often than not, your honesty will be received well, and your disciple will learn to trust you with an unwavering commitment.

There are, to be certain, limitations to our openness. Young people are intensely curious. You will often receive inquiries into your own sexuality and personal struggles. You might respond to your disciple in a general manner; never divulge information about yourself that is none of your disciple's business. In this case, you might smile and reorder the conversation: "This is about you, not me." This is not to say that your personal experience or parts of your story cannot provide a valuable lesson to your disciple. That is permissible, but personal details about moral struggles ought to remain your personal and untold story.

Integrity and Authenticity

The mentor can never be duplicitous: he cannot teach one thing and live another. The best practice is to be real. Never pretend to be someone you are not. Bragging about yourself or calling attention to yourself, unless in the context of teaching, will disillusion a disciple. He needs to know you with strengths and weaknesses unhidden, to learn from you and trust you—keeping in mind, as we have said, never to reveal information about yourself that a disciple need not know.

On the other hand, when it is appropriate, a disciple can learn much from your experience. You can certainly share your challenges, obstacles, and failures. But to go further, as if bragging about or even enjoying the recollections of past "exploits," is not productive. If a disciple urges you to reveal stories from your past, it is better simply to smile and move the conversation back to the disciple. He will understand.

To safeguard integrity in the mentor-disciple relationship, a simple personal principle is recommended: never ask a boy or a young man to do something that you would not be willing to do. For example, we might require a boy or a young man to dig a ditch while up to his knees in mud and shivering in the cold; but to ridicule him and laugh at him in that moment is not manly, nor is it productive in a mentoring relationship. Such a situation could bear enormous fruit if the mentor pulled on his own boots and jumped into the ditch alongside the young man — ready to work. That is mentoring.

There is a legendary founder of a movement for Christian men who is a master at mentoring. He has taken hundreds of men into the wilderness of the American West to experience tough work and inspired prayer. These expeditions, accomplished for the National Forest Service, are physically, emotionally, and spiritually demanding for young men who may never have been exposed to such dangerous and challenging work. Following a backpacking hike of several miles to reach an assigned location, a base camp is established, and the work begins. Wake-up call is normally at 4:30 a.m. The leader works his men hard throughout the day. Forest Service personnel are typically amazed by all that is accomplished: clearing heavy brush, building switchbacks and natural bridges, cutting enormous fallen Ponderosa pines, cutting stone, and other heavy work. Only hand tools, such as the crosscut saw, are used, as the work is accomplished in a designated wilderness area where power tools are not permitted.

This leader of men possesses natural mentoring skills and knows when and how to push a man, how to correct him, and how to praise him. But most important, he is always, without fail, shoulder to shoulder with his men. He is leading, teaching, encouraging, sweating, grunting, pushing, and always engaging the work. He never stands by merely to supervise the activity. In a difficult situation, he can sometimes be heard saying, "I don't know if I would do that," which essentially means he would not ask another to do what he himself would not do. At the end of the day, he is as tired as the rest, having outworked most of his men, even though he may be forty years older. He sets the pace, and he sets the standard for work.

You should never challenge a disciple if you have not faced (or are not willing to face) the same challenge yourself. Where you have not enjoyed success, you should make that very clear, and pledge your commitment to your disciple, as he is the next one to tackle the challenge. If he is successful, it will be an opportunity for great praise on your part, as he will have succeeded at something you were unable to do.

Forthrightness

A mentor must possess the ability to communicate to his disciple with care and skill; he must be able to speak the truth directly and in charity. He must be consistently authentic and must never flatter or exaggerate. At times, this may be unsettling to a disciple, as the truth can often be challenging. But a disciple appreciates knowing where he stands, knowing when he has made a mistake, knowing when he could be doing better. Of course, this is not to be judgmental, but it is certainly honest. As part of a formation team, I have experienced occasions when inappropriate behavior or areas of growth for a candidate for the priesthood were identified, but no one on the team had the resolve to share these conclusions with the seminarian! When presented with the disciple's well-being and success in mind, these points of correction are typically welcomed and eagerly accepted.

A statement of fact directed to a disciple may need to be carefully couched. "I need to be honest with you" might precede the communication of a fact that needs to be brought to the fore. Care must be taken. If a true mentor-disciple relationship exists, the disciple may be far more burdened by the mentor's disappointment than he is about a mistake he may have made. This is a delicate process and should always be done with the disciple's good in mind. If a mentor is up-front and forthright in a correction or a challenge, the disciple will know conclusively the veracity of correction, praise, or encouragement. Young people are truly grateful for direct speech.

Every summer, chaperones and I would take a promising group of high school boys to the Blue Ridge Mountains. As we began the long drive, I would allow the boys to listen to the music of their choice—a considerable penance on my part. Eventually, I would assume control of the stereo and plug in my iPod and play music I enjoy: sacred music, epic soundtracks, Big Band music from the 1930s and 1940s, bluegrass, Beethoven, Mozart and other selections that young people seldom listen to today. After listening to a good amount of complaining and moaning, I would challenge them: "The only reason you listen to the music you own is because you are told, by the culture and by an entertainment industry—an industry that wants only your money—what you must and must not listen to. Nobody tells me what I am going to enjoy."

I delight in giving them the backstory of much of the music that I have, and I cannot remember a trip when the boys failed to ask for a copy of my iPod playlist when we returned home. And, I happily admit, I have learned to enjoy some of the music that the young men listened to as well. My candid and open assessment—frank, forthright, and to the point—was never ridiculed.

Finally, when a mentor corrects or discusses failure, he must provide a reasonable solution to the problem for the disciple. Verbally punishing a disciple without giving him an opportunity to address the problem approaches bullying.

I read about a college man who successfully interviewed with a Fortune 500 company. He spent weeks in training and was given an esteemed, high-profile position in the company, along with a corner office and a secretary. On his first day on the job, he made a mistake that cost the company five million dollars. He knew he was finished. He went home mortified and paced his darkened apartment while drinking heavily. But, in the morning, he decided to take responsibility: he sobered up, showered, put on a suit, and drove to work. When he arrived, he went straight into his boss's office, confessed his mistake, and suggested that, considering what had happened, he would resign his position and leave the company. His boss looked at him, scowled, and blurted, "Quit? I just spent five million dollars educating you; now get back to work."

Due to youth and inexperience, young people will make mistakes. Any mistake, be it personal or professional, can be either a disaster or an opportunity to learn. A mentor, being forthright, should never ignore a failure or sugarcoat the consequences. With patience, he should frankly consider the situation with his disciple, consider the costs and consequences of the action, and help the young man to develop a prudent strategy to correct the situation. A mentor's willingness to stand by his disciple, even when it is uncomfortable, will teach the young person an invaluable lesson in fidelity and commitment.

Commitment

Our society is characterized by broken promises, broken commitments, and broken relationships. If a mentor enters a relationship, it must be characterized by continuity and remain effective until the disciple discontinues the relationship. Too many of our young men have had fathers or teachers or priests enter their lives, only, for various reasons, to abandon them. The wounds and suffering this can cause is unimaginable. It communicates to the young men that they are not worthwhile, acceptable, or lovable.

A high school football player I mentored was caught drinking with his friends following an important team victory. Remarkably, and even though he was a vital part of the team, he was rightly dismissed by his coach. At this point, he was filled with shame and felt completely abandoned. As we had a previously scheduled appointment for which he did not show, I sent him an e-mail, copied to his father, and told him that I was waiting for him. He was incredulous. "You still want to meet with me?" came his reply. I had made a commitment to him, and I intended to honor that commitment. I posted back, "I am at the church." He must have violated several traffic laws, arriving within minutes, cautious, curious, afraid, and supremely hopeful.

I recall the sad story of a young college man who spoke to me of his parents' divorce. With the family gathered in the living room, the news was broken that the young man's father had decided to leave the family and pursue another woman in the neighborhood. The now desperate young man stopped his father as he walked toward the door and yelled, "Dad, fight for us! Fight for us!" His father paused for a moment, stepped around him, and left the house. No doubt, life is hard, and marriage is challenging. But we, whether father or mentor, would do well to remember those terrible words: "Fight for us!"

Many times, I have worked with young men who were dealing with very difficult personal circumstances or moral choices. I always hold my ground and hold them to the Christian moral standard. Following much experience, I am no longer surprised if the disciple "escapes" the relationship and is not seen or heard from for a while. Unfortunately, this probably means the young man has chosen to pursue, at least temporarily, choices that are destructive or certainly not worthwhile. Happily, he often returns. At that point, the two of us must discern and redefine the relationship. He must admit his fault and acknowledge the failure. We agree that this will never happen again. He is almost always invited back into the mentor-disciple relationship, further proving the stability of the previously made commitment.

Availability

Availability can be a challenge. We are all busy with deadlines and obligations. When a young person approaches you, however, especially when under significant stress or anxiety, he will learn much about your personal commitment to him by your immediate response. Changing your schedule and devoting your attention to your disciple will communicate your appreciation and concern for him and his success and welfare. This is not always easy. Many young people seem to awaken about the time the rest of the world goes to sleep. But staying with a disciple, even when it is late or inconvenient, will speak volumes to a young man. He can be made to understand that a particular case is an exception — you do not want this to become a habit — but your availability and your willingness to be involved will assure him of your integrity and concern. Gratefully, I have never known a young man to be unaware of the sacrifice I was making for him, even those struggling with narcissism.

A true father is always available to his sons and daughters. The same must be said about the mentor. By way of illustration, say that your disciple calls you and is anxious about a decision he must make or is uncertain about some question that plagues him. Hearing you say, "Let me clear my schedule so we can talk in the morning" will be so much more meaningful than, "Okay, I can see you a week from Friday, if everything goes well." Making yourself available to a disciple confirms your commitment to him and demonstrates that he is a priority in your life, not just a project. When I talk with young men today and ask them, "If you could have anything, what would you want?" you may be as surprised as I am when you learn that what they really want is "more time with my father." Every man mournfully remembers Harry Chapin's song and the message masterfully communicated in "Cats in the Cradle."

Many recall the old story of eight-year-old Henry Brooks, who spent a memorable day fishing with his father. Upon returning home, he wrote in his daily journal, "Went fishing with my father today, the most glorious day of my life." Thirty years later, Brooks still fondly remembered the day spent fishing with his father. Curious, as he was now in possession of the journal his own father kept, he thought to compare his journal entry with his father's. Thirty years prior, on the same day his son described as "glorious," his father had written in his journal: "Went fishing with my son, a day wasted." Sadly, his father obviously did not consider time with his son to be significant.

Vulnerability

Vulnerability does not come easily to most men. Have you ever wondered why your father rarely, if ever, said, "I love you"? To say "I love you" is to make yourself completely susceptible to another and—conceivably—recklessly exposed. After all, the question of whether we are loved is the preeminent question, the deepest, most meaningful question. It takes a genuine man to utter the simple words "I love you." A man must be secure enough in himself to withstand whatever response he receives. This takes great courage for many men. Nonetheless, as we shall see, it is one of the most important truths we communicate to another. I do not remember my father telling me that he loved me. He provided for us and protected us, which he considered enough to communicate his love. Not so. As challenging as it may be, there is nothing more important for a son, or a disciple, to hear from someone he respects and admires.

Vulnerability, as it also concerns us, is humility, an understanding of one's limits, and an openness to the possibility that one can be mistaken. It includes the ability to apologize, the ability to "correct" a poor or incorrect decision, and the commitment to make a bad situation better. Thus, a mentor openly admits his human limitations and his inability to be correct every time. Vulnerability requires a reserve of humility and will protect a disciple from our stubbornness or pride.

I once had a disciple take me to task. With great respect and honesty, he told me that I had done something that he believed contradicted the dignity of my person. I had spoken poorly with coarse language in a public setting. Yes, his admonishment made me angry (mostly with myself), and I even questioned interiorly why he should be correcting me. But his honesty and care were evident. I made an apology and a quick resolution to correct the situation, and I have appreciated him ever since.

When a leader of men fails in leadership and refuses to admit his limitations, when he disappoints and refuses to embrace his limitations and then requires his men to carry on without his making allowance, he causes his men to fall into disillusionment. This is common. You may have seen this in an employer who rails at his men for business failures but refuses to take any responsibility himself. This leaves his team angry, demoralized, and ineffective. The men on his team will often turn to alcohol, pornography, and other self-destructive behaviors. Men will follow a leader they love and respect into the realms of hell and fight without fail. Vulnerability is not a crack in the armor. Vulnerability is an honest assessment and goes a long way toward earning the respect of those we lead.

Awareness of Your Limitations

While attempting to assist another individual, one of the most important principles is to know when to refer that person to a priest, a professional counselor, or even the civil authorities. This does not mean you make the referral and then abandon the disciple. In most cases, a young person must be reassured that professional help is necessary and that the intervention carries no shame.

Your reassurance and the assistance given to a young person to help him find a good Christian counselor will help your disciple receive the care and attention he may need for healing. Staying close to him and offering your encouragement and support can open him to a new world of self-understanding. You can help your disciple to process the work he is doing with the counselor, and, yes, you can help monitor what the young person is being told.

I was privileged to work with a young man in his twenties who was referred to me by his sister because he was struggling with drug and alcohol abuse. From our conversations I detected that the young man was utterly perplexed as to why "someone like me" was interested in "someone like him." When the time

came, I leveled with him. "Mike," I said somewhat confronta-
tionally, "I have grown to appreciate you, and you are important
to me, and I am not about to sit by while you destroy your life."
I paused for a moment and then continued: "If we are going to
remain friends, you must go to rehab and get the help you need,
help that I am not able to give." He responded heroically and
went to rehab. We maintained contact by letter, and I visited
him, following the guidelines of the rehabilitation institution,
when it was permitted. By the grace of God and his incredibly
hard work, he completely turned his life around and is now a
model of citizenship and fatherhood.

You should also be familiar with state laws regulating sexual
deviancy. Due to the breakdown of the family and the failure of
so many parents, the possibility of sexual or chemical struggle is
common. If you become aware, for example, that your disciple
may have engaged a minor in sexual activity, or is being abused
himself, and you neglect to report that situation to authorities,
you will, more than likely, be held criminally responsible. Strict
attention should be given to guidelines provided by youth organizations in which you are involved. Today, these guidelines
feel more like restrictions, but it would be prudent to accept
the guidelines and adhere to them strictly. Great care should
be taken when there is talk of suicide, and your limitations in
dealing with such a threat should be recognized. Parents and,
when necessary, authorities must be contacted. In cases such as
these, and others, much rests on state law.

* * *

Never use these techniques or methods to manipulate or use
another individual. At the core of mentoring is a sacred relationship between the mentor and his disciple. The mentor must

always be governed by the welfare of his disciple. If, in any way, the relationship becomes an opportunity to benefit the mentor or threatens to harm the emotional, psychological, or sexual well-being of the disciple, the relationship must be discontinued.

Part 3

THE DISCIPLE

I live in a small part of a very large world, but I truly believe that all I teach about mentoring has universal application. Look to your left and to your right. Chances are that the boys there are pushed aside for an alternative agenda and forgotten, but they are still there.

Dealing with boys and young men is not easy, but never think that they are not worth your effort. They are failing today; that is plainly evident. Many factors, some intentional, some unintentional, have contributed to this situation. Probably the most effective tool that social engineers have used to advance their agenda is confusion. Confusion is being used to influence individuals and, on a larger scale, our communities. When good people are confused about issues, they tend to become overwhelmed, which leads to an unsettled apathy.

Consider the effect this has on our boys. They are aware of certain natural instincts that they are told are now obsolete. They are eager to be heroic but are given the path of mediocrity. Men who once inspired boys and young men are now defined by their failures and are banished from our history. Natural and time-proven family structures are now completely dismantled and celebrated as such. Today's boys live in a world that constantly tries to convince itself that blatantly obvious gender differences do not exist. Is it any wonder that the young are confused?

As we look at the disciple, we must consider external and internal factors.

6

Relevant External Factors

In addressing temptations, St. Thomas Aquinas wrote: "There is not much sinning because of natural desires.... But the stimuli of desire which man's cunning has devised are something else, and for the sake of these sins, one sins very much."[30] This is an astounding quote and can be even more troubling when you consider that St. Thomas wrote in the thirteenth century, when there was an absence of prevalent pornography, no drug culture, no video games or other electronic media, and so forth. One might even rewrite the words of the saint and use them on the social level by replacing the word "sin" with forms of the word "destroy": "There is not much destruction because of natural desires, but stimuli of desire which man's cunning has devised are something else, and for the sake of these destructive activities, one destroys much!"

The problem with these "relevant external factors" lies in the fact that young people have been made to think that most of these destructive activities are good and worthwhile and that the people who bring them these pursuits—movie stars, singers, sports figures, nonconformists, or insurrectionists—have

---

[30] *Summa Theologica*, II-II, Q. 142, art. 2.

the young people's personal welfare in mind. It requires great patience and skill to convince young people otherwise. Take the hip-hop culture, of which I admittedly know very little, but which has an immense following among boys today. I have had several young men tell me how personally unsettled they were when they finally paid attention to the lyrics of songs and actions of rappers—lyrics and actions too graphic and despicable to relate here. Yet young people are taken by them, believing these singers empower them to rebel against family and culture, opening them to a perceived higher status of nonconformity. Most young people do not realize that these cultural entities are using them for their money and for support of their political or social agendas. Thus, one must proceed slowly.

Essentially, a mentor must convince his disciple that these people whom he thinks are his friends are not really concerned about him at all. I remember when Ted Turner was promoting his new idea of MTV, combining music and video, back in the 1980s. Visiting a college campus, he was asked about his influence on teenagers. He is reported to have snapped back, "Look, I don't influence teenagers; I own teenagers"—a rare bit of honesty from a corrupt industry.

Sex Culture

Not much need be said about the destructiveness of the sex industry, as the evidence is all around us. Apparently, addiction to pornography has left men struggling with various forms of erectile dysfunction. Pornographers know two things: (1) men are aroused by what they see, and (2) the earlier a boy discovers pornography, the more addicted he will be as an adult. This has resulted in a more-than-4.5-billion-dollar porn industry. It is wrong to conclude that "men want pornography" (as the industry claims), since, in most cases, men (even nonreligious men) despise its debilitating presence in their lives. With the Internet culture, a man need not go looking for pornography, as the rubbish will inevitably come looking for him.

It would be wrong to conclude that all boys and young men are participating in illicit sexual activity, but it can safely be assumed that all men struggle in this area. Confusion and misunderstanding about human sexuality are pervasive. Whereas most would counsel mentors to refrain from entering conversations addressing sexuality, there does not seem to be a choice for a mentor truly concerned about his disciple. If we do not talk with our young men and instruct them about the sacredness of sexuality, we leave them to the demented teachings of the dark side of the culture. Consider current trends in our communities and universities. Women, to mimic the behavior of men, have been led to believe that sexual promiscuity and the "hookup culture" can benefit women as much as—as some believe—it has benefitted men. But this translates to a culture in which young men will oblige a willing woman with no intention of marrying her or caring for her on a long-term basis. Remember your grandmother's question: "Why buy the cow when you can get the milk for free?" Young men have adopted the despicable practice of sexual intimacy with a woman with the full intention of abandoning her when he decides it is time to consider marriage. Women, who subconsciously believe that the intimacy will result in marriage, are being desperately hurt.

Interior shame and isolation caused by illicit sexual activity can easily destroy a young man and lead him to more destructive choices. Youth need to be taught that sexual drive and passion are not evil or signs of poor character—as most boys believe. They must understand that the drive is natural, but that pornographers and others exploit something about men that is meant to be used for a good and worthy purpose. Sexual drive is an indication of growth and physical maturity and should not be considered shameful or somehow dirty. Men need to know that nature dictates the distribution of DNA to future generations, which is the reason young men are so pressed by sex. A man's body is relentless in fulfilling its natural purpose. God has raised man to the supernatural level, however, and has given him a new charge that can be achieved only in self-mastery and the marital bond of a sacred union. Use of our sexuality outside of this covenantal relationship can bring untold misery to a man or a woman.

Boys and young men are usually greatly relieved to have the freedom to discuss these issues with someone they trust and respect. Your poised and calm attitude during the discussion will communicate a naturalness and ordinariness toward the subject. Again, this discussion must never include specific failures on your part and must always be treated with great respect and wisdom. One must be very careful when discussing this topic with boys or younger men. If a boy has not been exposed to these activities, you do not want to be the one to introduce him to them.

Many times, men get tired of their involvement in this dehumanizing activity. Most men will readily exchange sensual enslavement if offered a blessed, valued, realizable freedom in self-mastery. You can offer a boy or a young man this freedom in exchange for the sacrifices he will have to make to be chaste. He needs to know that without freedom, a man cannot love; and if he cannot love, he is no longer a man. Chastity is possible but will be realized only through prayer (especially the daily Rosary), asceticism, and fraternity.

Many professionals are working to provide solutions to these contemporary problems. Here are some helpful sites, although

I do not recommend introducing a site to a disciple without thoroughly investigating it first.

- Reclaim Your Sexual Health (reclaimsexualhealth.com)
- Fight the New Drug (fightthenewdrug.org)
- Art of Manliness (nonreligious); *The Surprising Benefits of Marriage for Men* (artofmanliness.com)
- Exodus by Those Catholic Men (exodus90.com)
- The Chastity Project (chastityproject.com)
- Integrity Restored (integrityrestored.com)

Drug Culture

Unfortunately, we cannot assume that the young man with whom we are working has not had some damaging encounter with drugs and alcohol. Again, the drug culture is pervasive, and one need not go looking for the opportunity. This has become a national tragedy that is typically ignored today, until a movie star or a sports figure dies from an overdose. A flood of news stories typically follows the death of a celebrity, and then the topic is forgotten until it happens again. Even the best of our young people might have had experience with drugs—some as hardcore as heroin or cocaine. Prescription drugs seem to be the drug of choice today and are easily acquired from medicine cabinets, peers, or dealers.

To help someone overcome drug addiction or drug use, several things must be kept in mind. First, never talk with someone under the influence. You will be wasting your time; wait until the person is sober. Never give an addicted person money. In many cases, they must hit a wall before they seek help. Admit your lack of experience with drugs, if it is true, and do not attempt to give advice. To do so is to lose credibility. I often openly admit my own inexperience and allow the addict to teach me. If you do this, your disciple will oblige your request.

Even though the counseling industry has searched for alternatives, Alcoholics Anonymous and Narcotics Anonymous have been tried, tested, and found successful. If a young person comes to you with this problem, it is best to stay with him and support him, but demand ninety consecutive days of attendance at these meetings. He might offer the typical complaints: "Those people are creepy" or "I am not like them" and "This will not work for me." Stand your ground. You have much to offer, and your disciple knows this.

If he wants your help, he must help himself. This may also be a good time to refer him to a counselor who can assist you and your disciple. Be selective, as some can be extremely effective, while others may have good intentions but lack the appropriate skill.

Be on guard. Most addicted persons have a very difficult time telling the truth. When I work with an addicted person, I very rarely believe anything he tells me. I am comforted by the thought that it is the drug and not the disciple that is lying to me. I will often ask the blunt question "When was the last time you were high?" or "When was the last time you were intoxicated?" You must be able to read the disciple's nonverbal communication to determine the truth of his answer. At times, you may even need to communicate that you feel as if you are not being given the truth.

Most people who are addicted to drugs or alcohol will seek help when they are in trouble: following an arrest, a divorce, flunking out of school, a physical altercation, or having been kicked out of their home. This is often called a "jailhouse conversion" and will not generally change a person. True, this is a time when someone needs your help the most, but you do not want to become part of the problem. Deal with the immediate situation first without allowing yourself to be used. Having resolved that situation, begin the more earnest work of recovery.

Again, a trained counselor will be of immense value to you and your disciple.

Remember, you can offer a young person something that drugs or alcohol may have taken from him: his personal freedom. You may have to convince him of its worth, as, in his mind, he is being asked to give up much. One of the most effective means of prevention is noting your own independence from drugs or alcohol. Telling a young person "Just say no" is completely inadequate. The phrase makes drugs tantalizing. I never tell a boy or a young man that I am more powerful than drugs. I admit my fear that if I had tried drugs, I may have liked them, and I very well may have lost everything.

Video Games, Netflix, and Social Media

Do you want to be sure to lose an argument? Try telling a Millennial that playing video games is detrimental to his growth.

Not long ago, I published an article discouraging the use of video games. I had no idea what I was unleashing. The anger and contempt that followed my article was a brutal awakening. I have successfully convinced a good number of men to give up a multitude of vices, but all hell breaks loose if I suggest that it would be better for a man not to play video games.

Why is it detrimental to play video games?

First, men are made for much more: men are called by God to greatness. By greatness, I mean that we have but a few short decades to accomplish great feats of heroic and selfless service for our families, for our country, and for our Church. When we consider that we are to be heroic (and, I understand, nobody talks this way anymore), we simply do not have time for empty activities such as playing video games or watching endless hours of Netflix.

Yes, of course, games can be entertaining and a source of relaxation. Companies have addressed criticism and made games more physical or even, via the Internet, more social.

Despite these developments, however, as men, we must live deliberately. We must live in such a way that the thought of spending valuable time on such activities would never cross our minds. Video games are a form of escapism, hiding from reality. At best, this is a waste of time; at worst, it is a distraction from the pressing needs of life. In many ways, it is like getting drunk — not just having a drink, but getting drunk. A man is not gaining perspective or being edified (as one does with a book, a good film, time with others, and so forth); he is disappearing into oblivion. The purpose of recreation is rejuvenation through activity that better equips one to engage the reality of one's life. Video-game and Netflix binges are about rejection of reality. This is not rejuvenation, nor is it recreation. A palpable despair seems to be present when one is involved in these activities.

You may very well lose this argument, but the argument must be made. Remember two things. First, we should help young men to consider alternatives to video games and offer activities that will contribute to young men's excellence as men. For example: Has your disciple ever backpacked the Appalachian Trail or the Great Continental Divide Trail? Learned a foreign language or a musical instrument? Competed in a sport? Has he ever gone fishing in a remote lake in Canada that can be accessed only by a pontoon plane? Has he mastered basic auto mechanics and learned to change the oil in his car and so forth? Has he walked the battlefields of Gettysburg, Shiloh, Chickamauga, Little Bighorn, and Yorktown, among others? Has he worked, earned money, and backpacked across Europe or Asia? Has he worked with the Missionaries of Charity to serve the poor? Has he joined the Knights of Columbus or other Catholic men's organizations?

What about astronomy, physics, archaeology, paleontology, geology, and so forth? Has he visited the residents of a local nursing home or veteran's home or spent good time with grandparents? (The elderly have much to teach.) Has he been trained in firearms or gone hunting? Has he spent a few days in a monastery? Has he read Dostoyevsky, Steinbeck, Hemingway, Tolstoy, or other amazing authors? Has he ridden his bike to California or to Washington, D.C.? Has he formed a fraternity of his peers to be mutually challenged for greater personal excellence? Has he sought an advanced educational degree? Has he dedicated time to the gym to lose weight or add muscle?

Why would a man squander his youth or his valuable time when there is so much to experience and there are so many to serve? When this list of pursuits was published for young men to read, some reacted with a boyish rant. "These activities are impossible" and "Nobody can do these things." Yet many do. Men must be intentional and use such formational experiences to build enough confidence to answer for themselves the fundamental question: "Do I have what it takes?" That question will not be answered sitting in front of a computer console or a television screen. A man is simply emasculated when he lacks these fundamental experiences.

Second, think about another example. The economy has shifted, and there is an extremely competitive job market with which to contend. Consider an employer who is interviewing candidates for a higher paying job or a worthwhile, exciting promotion. Would he hire a man who has been involved in some of the activities described above or one who has been playing video games? A game designer recently reported that, *on average,* twenty-one-year-olds have spent 10,000 hours playing video games. That is 1,250 eight-hour days or 3.4 years! Which man would you hire?

About so many who immerse themselves in video games, we often hear, "He is a boy; this is what boys do." Young men, especially, need to be pushed to experience life-changing adventures.

You will probably sound judgmental when you make such an argument, but your disciple must be made to think. Sometimes I think that to waste a life in such a manner is sinful. We are given only a small amount of time to live, and we must use that time wisely. There is not one person who does not have some important work to accomplish. We all have so much life to live. We have tasks to achieve that are reserved to us personally by God.

You may need to convince a young person that he was made for much more than he realizes. Have him consider the dark character Wormtongue in the epic story *Lord of the Rings*. This sycophant sat strategically close to Théoden, the great king of Rohan, and whispered debilitating nonsense into his ear. At a time when his kingdom needed him the most, Théoden was deceived by the incapacitating voice of a traitor and was rendered personally devoid of the power to act. It took the blow of the wizard Gandalf's staff to break the spell and set the king free.

In much the same way, video games distract people from what is real and from what must be done. You may need to help your disciple overcome this deception and allow him to reassert himself.

Organized Sports

Some may be surprised or even angry to see organized sports on this list. I will not condemn sports per se: the love of competition and the positive effects sports can have in the life of a boy or a young man are enormous. The principle to remember is important: sports are a means to an end, not the end itself. Sports can improve physical health, teach teamwork, build character, deliver a worthy test, and provide much satisfaction in a young man's life. Belonging to a team can provide unlimited benefits to a boy or a young man, and nothing can replace the experience of sports, as is evident in the collective memory of men.

As we have already noted, the universal question that all men must ask is "Do I have what it takes?" Thankfully, the arena of sports remains one of the most important venues in which a man can address this question. The most formative experience of a man's life may be the time spent with peers on a neighborhood diamond or basketball court or as a part of his high school or college sports team.

Sports can and should be a defining experience in a boy's life. On the other hand, too often, coaches are more concerned with winning and parents with scholarships than with building a young man's character. I have known some boys who have leveraged their entire existence and future on the pursuit of a sport. Rather than contributing to their overall character and their status as men, sports became limiting factors, taking essential time and energy away from other worthwhile and necessary pursuits. A teacher in a Georgia high school reported that, for several of his students, a mandatory twenty-hour week was reserved for their sports. This is the equivalent of a part-time job. In addition, punitive laps were required for high school men who elected (nonhabitually) to miss a practice to be involved at church. There is also the grievous development of missing one's Sunday obligation to attend sporting events.

We must also keep in mind that some are not as athletic as others; some may not be as interested in sports as others; and some may not be as physically gifted as others. A young man cannot measure himself only by his ability to perform on the court or on the field. Many try to do so, sometimes with disastrous results.

A young man related this story to me. As a member of a well-known college football team, he was enjoying great success, and his reputation around the nation was growing, until he sustained an injury. His world was shattered when he was redshirted and replaced by another member of the team. I met him five years later, and he was still reeling from the experience.

Another young man once tried desperately to play baseball. When he was a boy, he considered the ability to play the sport effectively to be the measure of a true man. But since he personally failed at the game, he questioned his own masculinity and, over time, began obsessing about the men who succeeded. He later concluded that this circumstance contributed greatly to, if it was not the sole cause of, his same-sex attraction. Many men have lamented the lack of instruction or coaching prior to trying out for a sport. With so many single-parent homes, this is all too common in our day. Pitting one boy against another in a competitive sport without proper preparation is nearly cruel.

We must work hard not to allow a "good" to become something malevolent. There is much to be gained from the proper engagement in sports. A young man once told me how he was astonished when he was invited to join a college football team. Although anxious about his prospects, he was utterly transformed by the generous support offered by his fellow teammates, who selflessly provided him with feedback and instruction. He told of teammates who truly wanted him to succeed and worked with him to make that happen. Of course, there were some who could not see past the competitive nature of the sport, but that did not overshadow the healthy and formative experience this became for the young man. By his own admission, he grew exponentially "as a man" during this time with the team.

The Education System

Nobody seems to see education as a privilege and a vocation anymore. Since the federal government or local states now fund much of education, its purpose has changed drastically in the modern era. Training in virtue, acquisition of wisdom, and growth of the human person have pretty much been abandoned, while efforts are now concentrated solely on job training. The state does not invest in young people for the sake of the young people themselves. The Christian anthropology that once undergirded educational efforts no longer exists. Today, universities and colleges are motivated by the prospect of raising the next generation of successful taxpayers.

Young people are not taught to think and to reason; they are taught to conform to a biased social and political agenda. Institutions that pride themselves on tolerance and openness are often anything but tolerant and open. Many speakers with a traditional worldview are often ostracized, and students are encouraged to protest such campus visitors publicly rather than thoughtfully consider their views. Instruction is devoid of any Christian influence or underpinning.

Fun

Nobody would begrudge a young person's need or desire to have fun. But when a young person gauges every activity, every pursuit, and even his career on whether it is "fun," he dramatically limits himself and his personal growth. This does not seem to be a problem solely attributable to our modern culture. St. Thomas Aquinas, commenting on Aristotle, noted that "it seems possible that the playful type, i.e., one too much in love with amusement, is intemperate because there is a kind of pleasure in amusement; the Philosopher says that such a person more properly is effeminate. Amusement is a quieting and relaxation of the mind, which the lover of amusement seeks to an excessive degree. Hence, he comes to the classification of effeminate, whose characteristic is to shun difficulties and labors."[31]

Young people must be encouraged to persevere in projects and activities that seem, on the surface, to lack the aspect of fun. Several articles have been published recently that encourage fun in the workplace. "To keep millennials," the periodical *Entrepreneur* once suggested, "offer flexibility and fun."[32] But how much would any person achieve if, at the first sign of difficulties or labors, he abandoned the pursuit of the objective and simply quit? Most of the truly satisfactory and rewarding experiences of life require an unwavering discipline and an immense amount of hard work.

A young man told me that he wanted to do "fun things" and that life was not about the drudgery of work. He even told me that, at the age of twenty-five, he was considering joining a traveling circus because it sounded like fun. When I told him that growing up and being a man with worthwhile responsibilities could be fun, too, he gave no response.

Another young man, a member of the U.S. Navy, lamented new recruits who wanted to quit the armed forces because they

---

[31] Thomas Aquinas, *Commentary on Aristotle's Nicomachean Ethics*, trans. C. I. Litzinger (Notre Dame, IN: Dumb Ox Books, 1964), 1417.

[32] Doug and Polly White, "What to Expect from Gen-X and Millennial Employees," *Entrepreneur*, December 23, 2014, https://www.entrepreneur.com/article/240556.

were not having fun. Tackling a job, a project, or a cause for its own sake can be rewarding and supremely fulfilling—and very instructive.

Boys and young men should be praised and rewarded for good grades, reading, earning money, athletic achievement, reaching personal goals, contributing to their communities, and accepting sacrifices designed to make them better men. I learned this lesson well on our small farm when I was a boy. Raising 100- to 200-pound feeder calves to 1,200 or 1,300 pounds required early-morning feeding, a consistent supply of water (even when it would freeze in the winter), clean barns, and a good amount of attentive care. But I soon learned that the result, the success of the effort, was an invaluable and irreplaceable feeling of accomplishment.

7

RELEVANT INTERNAL ISSUES

Homosexuality

The topic of homosexuality would be easier simply to put aside, as the topic is fraught with emotion; but that would be cowardly. Many have already adopted the views and the doctrine of the homosexual lobby and are set in their belief. Not much will change their conviction. I accept that and ask only for a thoughtful and respectful hearing of what is presented here, and that consideration be given to this issue within the greater context of this book: that all men are brothers and most lack, in varying degree, proper human development within the context of what it means to be male.

Homosexuality seems to be increasing — some would say due to a more tolerant social view, while others point to the breakdown of the family. Statistica reports that 2.2 percent of the population "identify as gay in the United States."[33] Other studies report 10 percent, 3.5 percent, 2.0 percent — much depends on the working definition of "homosexuality" and, unfortunately, the political agenda of those compiling the research.

---

[33] "U.S. Homosexuality: Statistics and Facts," Statistica, 2017, https://www.statista.com/topics/1249/homosexuality/.

The culture is presently attempting to convince itself that homosexuality is acceptable and natural. No matter how politically correct society considers homosexuality to be or how much it is promoted through social marketing, its acceptance — especially by many who "struggle" with same-sex attraction — is doubtful.

A young man once told me, "I would not wish homosexuality on my worst enemy, but I would not give it up for anything in the world." This is indicative of the confusion young men discover in the homosexual culture.

In the silent mainstream are countless young men who struggle with same-sex attraction but do not consider homosexuality to be useful, natural, or a means to happiness. Alongside homosexual men who have made their sexuality public are hundreds of thousands of young men who are repulsed by such behavior and seek self-mastery, self-understanding, and healing. They suffer greatly with same-sex attraction and the countless difficulties associated with it. No amount of societal doublespeak or politically correct talk changes that for them.

Prejudice?

Yes, prejudice exists, but the greatest bigotry is directed toward the homosexual man who considers same-sex attraction to be a disorder and seeks healing. California and New Jersey have outlawed therapy that attempts to help individuals overcome homosexuality.

Even now, nobody truly knows why a man might experience same-sex attraction. The epic failure of a great amount of effort to find a biological reason or a gene that causes homosexuality is revelatory. Equally revelatory is the common background shared by most homosexual men: a harsh, uninvolved father who never seems to "delight" in his son; an inability to interact with peers of the same sex; a controlling mother; emotional neglect, abandonment, overwhelming feelings of inadequacy; and especially hatred toward his father (who might be an alcoholic, uninterested, or have pursued a woman other than his mother). Although many would deem these issues irrelevant, they seem to be a common experience among homosexual men. The result is often a total lack of self-acceptance, or even more, a self-hatred (even before the onset of sexual awareness).

In some ways, the homosexual man shares this experience with the heterosexual man. All men are concerned about their status as men—whether they are true and worthy men. The homosexual man, however, often becomes obsessed with the question.

What can be done for a young man struggling with same-sex attraction? Sadly, if the situation is not addressed before puberty, the possibilities are limited. He may always struggle with same-sex attraction. But what can be done is evident: experience shows that the more integrated into the "masculine culture" a man becomes, the less dependent he becomes on same-sex fantasies and attractions. As St. John Paul II taught, men are attracted to mystery, especially the mystery of the opposite sex. However, when a young man feels alienated toward his own gender, masculinity itself becomes a mystery and, unfortunately, becomes emotionally and sexually attractive.

A homosexual man, outside this community of men, finds himself "looking at men" rather than standing side by side with them. That position quickly leads to self-condemnation. He eventually begins to fantasize about men as if a same-sex encounter can correct his feeling of inadequacy. Obviously, this will not work and will lead to countless sexual encounters.

If, however, he is invited into the community of men and mentored appropriately; if he is treated as an equal; and if he sees himself accepted, supported, and even loved by that community, he will be less likely to fantasize and long for things of men. Men and the world of men will no longer be a mystery to him.

Unfortunately, much of the research and study of homosexuality has been derailed by a very intolerant and combative homosexual lobby not interested in exploring the truth. Current research by Catholic therapists is bearing much fruit. A good Christian counselor, not bent on reparative therapy or, alternatively, the acceptance of the lifestyle, will be a necessity for healthy self-acceptance and for coping with same-sex attraction. Care should be taken to find a balanced counselor with a Christian anthropology and a Christian framework within which to work. Otherwise, the results may be disastrous.

More important and more effective is the work of the father. A father who truly affirms and accepts his son, who teaches him and supports him, who relishes him, who spends good time with him and is careful not to belittle him, who wrestles with his son and is physical with him, who claims his son even when his son fails, has all the power necessary to raise a healthy and happy man.

Narcissism

Many people attack young people today with the accusation that the entire generation is narcissistic. People seem blind to the fact that most of us are narcissistic. Narcissism chokes true growth in a person, replacing a pure desire for true greatness with a desperate attempt at attention and acceptance. Narcissism also utterly disrupts the mentoring process and makes progress all but impossible. The narcissist is concerned with other people's opinions; he is desperate for love and affirmation; and he needs others to convince him of his greatness. A narcissist will always present himself at his best: he is typically well-dressed, well-groomed, physically fit, and handsome by most measures. Gregarious and eager to be the center of attention, he volunteers and takes an active part. He is personable and makes friends easily; he is seemingly successful and full of potential. He is the young man whom everyone loves to love. That makes sense, as he has spent an enormous amount of effort to "be someone" and to acquire (not earn) significance.

On the other hand, he is all for show. In reality, he is attempting to convince himself that it is good that he exists. Interiorly, he does not believe that he has the aforementioned characteristics. He wants the title and the corner office but will do little to earn the privilege. He desires to associate with "important people," as he knows the association will benefit him. He harbors fantasies about being a hero but will not work to build the necessary character or skill. Perhaps most detrimental, he may not even realize he harbors latent self-hatred.

It requires a good amount of careful discernment to determine whether a disciple is authentic or narcissistic. To mistake a narcissist for a truly magnanimous person is demoralizing. Having freely invested in a person, a mentor is not likely to see any meaningful fruit, as the narcissist simply takes all he can and then moves on to someone he perceives as greater, someone who can do more for him.

The *Diagnostic and Statistical Manual of Mental Disorders, Fourth Edition* (2000) states that a pervasive pattern of grandiosity indicated by answering positively to five of the following criteria would indicate clinical narcissism: a grandiose sense of self-importance; preoccupation with fantasies of unlimited success, power, brilliance, beauty, or ideal love; belief that he is "special" and unique and can be understood only by, or should associate only with, other special or high-status people (or institutions);

a desire for excessive admiration; a sense of entitlement; a tendency to be interpersonally exploitative; a lack of empathy (an unwillingness to recognize or identify with the feelings and needs of others); envy of others or the belief that others are envious of him; arrogant, haughty behaviors or attitudes.

Assistance provided by a professional therapist may be required if your disciple self-identifies with these categories. Helping a narcissistic person admit the need for therapy, on the other hand, can be quite difficult.

There are two varieties of narcissism to consider: grandiose and vulnerable.

Grandiose narcissism is what most people have experienced as narcissism. The grandiose narcissist has been led to believe that he is as great as he thinks he is or wants to be. This individual is very difficult to interact with. He has an inflated sense of self-worth; he truly believes he is superior in many ways and only tolerates the incompetence of those around him. His thoughts are loftier, his conclusions more definitive, and his skills unmatched. He believes himself to be more charming, more successful, and physically more appealing than his peers. The grandiose narcissist is likely to very abusive in his relationships, especially with wives or girlfriends whom he believes do not measure up to his standards or expectations. Presenting children with trophies for participation, granting good grades without commensurate work, and giving extravagant presents for no reason are great ways to form a grandiose narcissist.

Far more prevalent, but hard to detect, is the vulnerable narcissist. This narcissist desperately scrambles for love and affection and validation from others. He may conceal his inner longing to be a person of greatness and superhuman destiny, but it rules his life.

Sadly, my experiences show that this narcissist often seems to be the son of a mother who uses her children for her own emotional fulfillment, rather than supporting and shaping them. These women "own" a child as most of us would own a pet. Most people purchase a dog or a cat to make them happy and to bring them a certain satisfaction. When a mother regards her son as a pet, he must spend the rest of his life trying to convince himself that "it is good that I exist" for his own sake. Such a mother vehemently controls and manipulates her son to bend him to her will, her dreams, and her priorities. Ironically, a narcissist's father is typically passive—just the sort of man a controlling woman needs. He does little to intervene or correct the mother-son relationship.

The result, following years of such emotional abuse, is a broken individual who is not capable of having a healthy sense of self. Although he craves love and affirmation, he has trouble receiving them. For example, many vulnerable narcissists are sexually promiscuous. They do not believe in their own worth, but they search desperately for that person who can "affirm" them—and affirmation attempted via a sexual encounter is toxic. Again, the result is devastating. More than one man has described the need to have the most beautiful woman in the bar clinging to his arm as he tries to convince the world that he is important and valuable.

A mentor must take care not to be used by a narcissist, whether grandiose or vulnerable. If the mentor is an important figure or a well-known member of the community, a narcissist may cling to him to promote himself. He is likely to mine the relationship for anything of value and then, when he has taken all that he can, abandon the mentor. Therapists often claim that the only way to healing for a narcissist is to "hit the wall" (academic failure, a divorce, or a business failure) and to be devastated in some manner—this seems to serve as a reality check that can spur authentic living.

The mentor must focus on holding the narcissist accountable. The narcissist must begin to notice that he is manipulating people or situations to his own selfish benefit, and when he realizes this, he must make a courageous act of the will to change his behavior. To believe he will be free of this narcissistic tendency is usually futile—it will, more than likely, follow him throughout life.

Classical Effeminacy

Classical effeminacy is the result of a rudderless and senseless culture. The term "snowflake," often bandied about these days, may be a contemporary take on an ancient category. Classical effeminacy is evident when a man, having set his goals and begun striving for personal excellence, lacks the ability and stick-to-itiveness to persevere and bring an effort to its conclusion. As understood by St. Thomas Aquinas, classical effeminacy is the antithesis of perseverance. A man characterized by classical effeminacy does not seem to have the wherewithal to withstand any opposition or challenge; he is a man "ready to forsake a good on account of difficulties which he cannot endure."[34] A young man needs support and must be given opportunities to prove, mostly to himself, that effort, work, and perseverance will pay off in the end. Life must demonstrate to him that he can conquer and prevail. Time and time again, I have encountered young men with great potential who, having exerted themselves in some small degree, will conclude, "It cannot be done" or allow themselves to be distracted by some other, more tantalizing, pursuit.

[34] *Summa Theologica*, II-II, Q. 138.

When I was a teenager, my family and I lived in a rural area of Illinois. Most of my friends were farmers, and finding work was relatively easy. One very hot afternoon, a farmer I worked for announced to his hands that we were to bale a 250-acre field of clover hay. Clover hay, as I remember it, was heavy and scratchy and, after a day in the field, left your lungs filled with chaff. Thunderstorms were in the forecast, and the farmer was desperate to get the hay into his barn.

Resourceful, he contacted the coach of the high school wrestling team with the promise of a sizable donation if his team would work to get the hay stacked in the barn. Now, I was a tall, skinny boy, and the thought of muscle-bound wrestlers truly intimidated me. When they arrived, everyone was given a place and a task. By the heat of the sun and the humidity in the air, it was evident that this was not going to be fun. The tractor thundered, and the familiar sound of the baler's plunger responded in rhythm. At least we would make quick work of the field, or so I thought. After the tractor finished its first pass over the field, the entire team abandoned the work and headed home. I was dumbstruck. I found it inconceivable that many of these young men were content with their decision and seemed utterly justified in giving up the effort. Deserting the objective because it was too difficult or not fun did not seem to cause them any humiliation. Such men, not too long ago, would have been considered effeminate or delicate and an undesirable employee or friend.

Based on my extensive involvement in ministry to men, I realize that many will not appreciate what is written here. After all, they might conclude, "What does it matter if a boy or a young man approaches life casually—content with himself and comfortable in his performance? Who are you to judge his intentions or effort?" Such a response sets the stage for failure and promotes mediocrity. No well-adjusted man can be satisfied with mediocrity. When life becomes difficult and unmanageable — and it will — a man prone to classical effeminacy will wilt before us.

I have preserved the following anecdote, mostly as a reminder to myself, about the mediocrity to which classical effeminacy can lead. The story is about the first king of the Holy Roman Empire, Charles the Great, or Charlemagne, who united most of Western Europe in the Middle Ages. Derek Wilson wrote of him:

> He was at court when some of his courtiers arrived back from Pavia, where they had been enjoying the festival and returned flaunting fashionable clothes of silk, bedecked with feathers and ribbons. Charles insisted that they immediately accompany him on a hunting expedition. The poor men were given no time to change and for several hours were obliged to ride through forest glades and thickets, lashed by rain and briars. On their return they were not allowed to change out of their bedraggled finery. Charles kept them dancing attendance upon him till late into the night. The next morning their ordeal was not over, for Charles commanded them to present themselves in the same clothes they had worn the day before. As they stood before him, shivering in their tattered, muddy garments, the king pointed out to them the moral of their uncomfortable experience: they should not allow their manhood to be sapped by effeminate, debilitating luxury.[35]

By way of examination, a mentor would do well to identify in his disciple any sign of effeminacy and to assist him in rooting it

---

[35] Derek Wilson, *Charlemagne: A Biography* (New York: Doubleday, 2006), 132.

out. This can only be done effectively with patience, understanding, and appropriate encouragement. Most men who employ youth know that young people who were raised on farms seem to be immune to classical effeminacy. There is no room for such a characteristic when the success of the family depends on the success of the farm. If you encounter a young man who knows how to work or persevere, it is likely that he grew up on a farm or in a family that owns a construction company or another business that requires hard work. These young people have spent their lives learning to persevere.

Know the signs of classical effeminacy, and help your disciple to recognize them: avoidance of physical work or physically challenging activity; an oversensitivity or lack of firmness toward oneself, or a tendency to make allowances for oneself; a lack of initiative; oversubmissiveness or docility; overly domesticated behavior; inhibitions; narcissism; pleasure seeking; feelings of inferiority; lack of self-control (especially with lust); unwarranted pride; disproportionate self-love; and lack of self-discipline.

Emotional Deprivation

Obviously, our society has changed dramatically over the past fifty years. The family, it must be acknowledged, is in disarray. Parenting children is no longer a respectable and valued prerogative in a society given to money, fun, and professional success. Whether we want to admit the fact or not, many young people are emotionally and psychologically impoverished. On her news program, an anchorwoman, having recently given birth to a child, congratulated herself on "being back in the chair in front of the camera less than three weeks after leaving the hospital." This might have worked well for her but had to be devastating to her child.

Even more, many mothers have reported the condemnation they have received from others because they chose not to pursue a career outside the home. If we are going to overcome widespread human desolation, our society must examine the way we raise our children. Would that we lived by a simple maxim regarding children: if you have them, raise them! No one would begrudge a man or woman who desires to pursue a career or an avocation. But when will we admit to ourselves that child rearing is far too important to be shared with other pursuits? Otherwise, we are simply condemning our children by depriving them of all that is necessary for happy living and perhaps even eternal salvation.

The consequences are ugly. By way of analogy, consider the situation as such: Everyone is born with a wooden "bucket" that is somewhat damaged and has a hole in the bottom. The hole varies in size from bucket to bucket. Every bucket has the capacity to carry some amount of water, but because of the hole, water drips or trickles or, in some cases, pours out the bottom of the bucket. The water must be replenished.

The same can be said of the need for human love. Obviously, a human person can receive love, but because of man's wounded human nature, we are broken and often find it difficult to hold the love given. And depending on one's upbringing, the size of the hole in the bucket varies from person to person. That said, one of the most difficult cases to consider is a person who is so greatly wounded, so very troubled, that his bucket does not even seem to have a bottom. No matter the amount or quality of love given, it cannot be received or held. This person can only take and take with little capacity to return. This is more common than one would expect—and more devastating than one might imagine.

You may have to accept that you do not have the where-withal to help such a person. The best that can be attempted is to help the individual realize his insatiable need for love and to help him accept his brokenness. Awareness and acceptance will help him to move beyond seizing love and clinging to anyone who is present and capable of giving love. Clinging and seizing serve only to push people away, and in the person's loneliness, the difficulty perpetuates itself. In most of these cases, even a professional will not be able to do much for the person. The cure for such a dilemma is prevention, and this will be covered as we look at the skill of mentoring.

Impulsivity and Lack of Discipline

Discipline is largely absent among our young people today. Older adults can be very judgmental toward younger generations for their lack of discipline and their disorderly conduct. Here we see, once again, the essential need for mentoring among young people. Lack of discipline is hardly their fault, and it would be unjust to hold them to a lofty standard about discipline. After all, our society has raised them to be who they are. The equivalent would be using a donkey to run against a quarter horse. There is no match. The expectation of discipline from a member of the millennial genera-tion is ridiculous, as we have neglected to teach them or provide adequate experiences and accountability where discipline can be learned. Absent training in discipline, what could be a magnificent quarter horse turns out to be a lanky donkey.

The most destructive response we can have toward those who lack discipline is to condemn them for what they lack. If there is some fault in the young people around us, we must look at our-selves first. We are their mentors, and we must take responsibility for these shortcomings and character flaws.

Discipline can be immensely beneficial to our young people and should not be considered a negative experience. "For the moment all discipline seems painful rather than pleasant; later it yields the peaceful fruit of righteousness to those who have been trained by it" (Heb. 12:11).

Discipline must always be for the good of the disciple and never a vying for power or control between the disciple and the mentor. You cannot tell a boy how to become a man; he must be shown. The best way is to give a young man a task or a project for which he is responsible. If he fails, you must sit with him and analyze his work and the effort he put forth. Help him to evaluate his failure. If he succeeds in the task, you must help him see that the work he has completed was done well and praise him for the fruit his effort has born.

Related to discipline is impulsivity—something that will never (and should never) be eradicated in the life of a young man. Impulsivity has roots in our evolutionary history. Elders of the tribe throughout history have always called upon young males to prove themselves and demonstrate their physical ability—long before the enemy or famine arrives. And the elders were not the only members of the tribe interested in this activity; young females were close by, watching and judging the young men's exploits in search of a worthwhile companion. The same remains true today, although many people consider these customs juvenile and sophomoric. Young women might laugh and roll their eyes at dangerous feats performed by young men, but the practice has been observed in every generation.

What do you do with young men compelled by nature to prove their skill and physical worth? At its worst, this call of nature degenerates into risks featured on such ridiculous television programs as MTV's infamous *Jackass*, which tend to carry this risk taking to a brainless extreme. Impulsivity must always be balanced by prudence.

Hiking the wilderness in the mountains of West Virginia, my peers and I once came upon an abandoned ranger station with a platform many feet above the base of the station. Without a word, an air of excitement spread through our group, and up we went. The metal ladder creaked, and the entire structure swayed in the wind.

Impulsive, maybe even reckless, but the experience was hugely formative. Everyone benefited from the trial, and my peers felt a sense of triumph. This impulsive behavior, balanced with prudence, was able to provide a sense of self-awareness and self-understanding.

Part 4

THE PROCESS

In 2012, in one of his last official statements before abdicating, His Holiness Pope Benedict XVI spoke prophetically to the Roman Curia on Christmas. Commenting on the contemporary human condition, he anxiously lamented, "It is now becoming clear that the very notion of being—of what being human really means—is being called into question." A society bent on eliminating gender differences and reordering social roles and relationships has wrought havoc on our young people, who are now confused and intentionally disconnected. Many of us seem to be aware of the impoverishment that follows such nonsense, but few of us feel equipped to address the situation. The pontiff was left cold and worried by the now celebrated development of these new human values. "From now on," he warned us, "there is only the abstract human being, who chooses for himself what his nature is to be."

The implications are far reaching, and the impact is overwhelming, especially for men. Rather than entering a sacred realm—as men have done for ages—and assuming the role demanded of him by nature, a young man is left with the "freedom to create himself," which is exactly why men have become selfish, self-centered, confused, domesticated, and lost.

We need young men to be strong and self-mastered and ready to contribute to the family and society. Nevertheless, in too many fields, current societal paradigms have nearly eliminated the role of young men in our society. Few today would question the sincerity and accomplishments of women, but in many fields, the movement of women intent on replacing their male counterparts is harmful if not disastrous. To a great extent, success so far has been due largely to a lack of societal stress. The success enjoyed by women in fields such as the military, construction, law enforcement, and so forth has not really been tested. Should some destabilizing event occur on a national level—an event that threatens the very existence of the people or at least a large fraction of the people—we will see nature dictate the reordering of traditional societal roles, to the benefit of us all. The struggle for survival will require men and women to maximize their potential by returning to the roles dictated by their ever-prevailing nature.

In his last address, Pope Benedict quoted the "famous saying" of the existentialist philosopher, political activist, and writer Simone de Beauvoir (1908–1986) that became the rallying cry for modern feminists: "One is not born a woman; one becomes so." By this, she meant that women are not born "inferior" and "submissive" but are taught to be so, mostly for the pleasure and dominance of men. Beauvoir's disdain for nature and the natural order was so potent that she managed to derail society itself.

But she was gravely mistaken. In the natural order, an infant identifies so closely with his mother that mother and child form a unity or a dyad. This is a good place for a girl to be; but leaving this beautiful place, the boy is required to make a very long and arduous journey "into his own" as a man. Otherwise, he will spend the rest of his life on the outside, wondering why he is alienated from other men and his true self—frustrated, excluded, and forever feeling inadequate. The journey a boy is required to make begins with male mentoring, is directed by male mentoring, and is concluded with male mentoring.

Social engineers do not want this to happen, as it has the potential to overturn their agenda. A real hostility exists toward male mentoring, even on the local level, far from those directing the anti-male agenda.

The time has come to flip Beauvoir's statement that "one is not born a woman; one becomes so" and use it to emphasize the necessity of mentoring boys and young men. In fact, it is men who are not born, but made. We can no longer leave boys to themselves and expect them to be the type of men who are happy and fulfilled and ready to make worthy and significant contributions to our families, our country, and our church. If they are to become the men, true and natural, they were created to be, boys need to be patiently and methodically taught, nurtured, and, most especially, mentored. The time has come to begin anew to guide our boys to be good Christian men (and not be ashamed of that craft).

This creates a difficulty for most men who are interested in mentoring and willing to do it. Most men of our era were not mentored themselves and may never have seen mentoring in action. Many have no idea how to proceed or have not the wherewithal to mentor a young person. In our contemporary world, this skill has nearly been forgotten. Do not be afraid. With the guidance of this book and your natural instinct, the present generation of men may be the one to revive the practice of mentoring and develop practical ways to carry it out. The first step is for the mentor to trust himself.

8

PRELIMINARIES

Mentoring is extremely challenging and intensely difficult work. Because we are dealing with human beings, anything is possible. A disciple with whom you have worked may make choices, reach conclusions, or take actions completely counter to all you may have taught him. A disciple may listen to you only casually or may even challenge what you say. He may seek other individuals to counter or challenge what you are teaching him. He may fail in a truly epic manner. And he may anger you with his apathetic attitude and refusal to accept a challenge.

During your work together, he may disappear without an explanation and then reappear when he believes the relationship will benefit him in some way. He may leave your side to explore the dark side of our culture. He will certainly and without doubt test your resolve, and he will probably be suspicious or at least curious about your motivation. Investing in a young person can be as deflating as it is exhilarating.

And yet, when you can make a connection, he will astonish you with his growth and with the seriousness with which he takes your involvement. Although you think he has not been listening, you may later overhear him repeating your words in conversation with others. If he respects you, he will be eager to please you and will always seek your approval. He would rather die than disappoint you. He will be heroic and will confront hell if he knows you have his back.

Mentoring is a selfless task; it is an investment in the future—a future that you may never see. You may never know the good that you have accomplished; nor should you look for such a reward. Just when you believe that you have failed, your disciple will surprise you. Yes, mentoring will make you a better man, but for that to happen, you must be "man enough" to mentor a man.

Relationship is crucial to mentoring. This can be a challenge, as acting relationally does not come naturally to men. Boys and young men are not looking for a trainer or an adviser or a coach as much as they're looking for a father or a worthy friend. Being in relationship with a disciple will provide you with a much clearer assessment of your charge. If the relationship is to be generative, it must be grounded in sincerity, truth, commitment, disinterest, and selflessness. As such, before work begins, you must decide whether the disciple is worth your investment, whether he is worth the fight. This depends largely on whether he is willing to engage in a formation process. Once a relationship has been established, you are "in" and must remain so, until the disciple announces your relationship's end.

Admittedly, most men harbor great fear and anxiety at the thought of being "in relationship" with a young person. They loathe the possibility that others may question their involvement or misunderstand their connection to young people. The predator uses very sinister methods to entrap his victims. To ingratiate himself with a young person, a predator will mimic the mentor. The trust a disciple gives his mentor provides access to the young person, most especially to his interior life, with its unspoken needs and complicated emotions. As a result, a bystander can sometimes be mistaken and confuse the good intentions of a mentor for the evil intentions of a predator. Satan has played this very, very well.

Open communication with the disciple's parents, scrupulous adherence to prescribed protocol, and above-board behavior are essential to the mentor in protecting himself. Because false accusations are a real possibility, you must live and interact with your disciple with such integrity that an accusation would be utterly unbelievable. Then you must trust Divine Providence and the inherent goodness of people.

Before you say a word, you must listen, and then listen some more, and then listen again. Listen not only with your ears: study the young man intently, making connections, reading facial and body language, watching for anxiety, stress, sorrow, authenticity, enthusiasm, and the emphasis he places on important aspects of his life. Strive to understand him on an intimate level. You must rise above stereotypes when interacting with your disciple, and he must also be immune to stereotypical behavior. Young people do not like to be misunderstood and will passionately revolt against rash and inaccurate conclusions.

Under no circumstances should you belittle, mock, or ridicule your disciple. To do so would be to imitate a dysfunctional culture intent on destroying young men. Yes, discipline and correction will be necessary, but they are never done while losing sight of your disciple's dignity as a human being.

Years ago, a farmer in our community took an interest in a young man and, from all indications, was offering him much in the way of instruction, support, and mentoring. It soon became known, however, that the farmer was using demeaning forms of discipline, such as forcing the young man to hang by his arms from rafters in the barn for long periods. He was also harsh, if not verbally cruel, in his assessment of the young man and would often severely criticize the boy in the presence of other men. The young man would have been better off left alone.

Your disciple must be treated better. In many cases, your disappointment will be enough to correct inappropriate behavior.

9

THE MENTORING PROCESS

Modeling

If you wish to be of valuable assistance to your disciple, remember this: you cannot tell a boy how to become a man; you must show him. You can talk all you want. You may even impress him by your wisdom and experience. But if you are to change the life of a young man and set him on the road to mature manhood, you must stand with him, side by side, and guide him through the years of his youth. He should be required to undertake manual labor, physical challenges, charitable service, and a myriad of other formative activities; but for these activities to be effective, your disciple must do them alongside of you. You must set the pace and be the means whereby he can learn to push and challenge himself and negotiate the many difficulties of life, so that, at the end of the day, he can talk with you about all that was accomplished. It is a matter of learning from you as he spends time with you, interacts with you, and even studies you.

You can tell him to respect women, but showing him how you interact properly with women will far outweigh any word you give him. He must see and learn from you: from your actions, proper manners, perseverance, hard work, honesty, integrity, religious devotion, respect for other people, and so forth.

Many outwardly condemn the millennial generation and are critical of their inability to engage successfully in some of the most basic activities of life. Older generations have nearly written them off as an apathetic and useless generation of narcissists and talentless fools. When I was working on a team that formed men for the priesthood, I often cautioned the team not to condemn the seminarians and nitpick their faults. I reminded the team that we were models for the seminarians, and if the seminarians were not "measuring up," we had an obligation to look at ourselves as we were modeling for them.

Many young people want to succeed, and they have good intentions to do so. The problem is plain to anyone paying atten-tion: young people do not have the modeling that an apprentice needs for success. Young people are willing to learn, and they personally seek to succeed, but they lack training in human and professional formation. The failure of the millennial is not his fault; it is the fault of those who have come before him who are empowered to teach and model but have not done so.

Not long ago, feminists encouraged fathers to take their daughters to work — an excellent and very profitable idea. But nothing was offered for a father's son. I often wondered what a boy would think as he was left without such experiences. This attitude must change.

Basic professional etiquette, such as punctuality, responsibil-ity, perseverance, and initiative, and human characteristics such as empathy, compassion, integrity, and the ability to negotiate conflicts must not only be taught to boys but must also be clearly and frequently demonstrated for them.

Some experiences involve nonverbal mentoring, especially ones that a young man might not be able to accomplish on his own: domestic and international travel, fishing or hunting trips, auto mechanics, carpentry, and charitable service, as well as hiking, studying astronomy or natural history, visiting museums, and attending sporting events.

Young people are drawn to epic adventures. Your task is to take an epic adventure and make it a formative experience. For example, teaching a young man that the poor of our society deserve our support and our charity is worthwhile. But identifying a nearby struggling family or elderly couple in need of assistance and actively addressing their needs by providing food, home repairs and maintenance, or other important work can utterly change the life of a young man. Hiking to the top of a nearby mountain can be physically challenging and very appealing, but resting at the top of the mountain while discussing the surrounding beauty will open a young man's eyes to things he may never have seen before. Your appreciation and awe before creation will draw an equal response from your disciple.

The Essential Validation Requirement

The story of King David in the Old Testament provides a fantastic means by which to learn much about masculine life (1 Sam. 16:1–13). We can profit abundantly by contemplating David's manner of life and the legacy he left us. Saul, the first king of Israel, failed to keep God's commands and thus lost his throne. The prophet Samuel, who had anointed Saul as king, was dejected by his king's failure. The day soon came when the Lord said to Samuel, "How long will you grieve over Saul, seeing I have rejected him from being king over Israel? Fill your horn with oil and go; I will send you to Jesse the Bethlehemite, for I have provided for myself a king among his sons ... and you shall anoint for me him whom I name to you."

Samuel did what the Lord commanded and went to Bethlehem.

When he arrived, he looked on Eliab, Jesse's eldest son, and thought, "Surely the LORD's anointed is before me." But the Lord said to Samuel, "Do not look on his appearance or on the height of his stature, because I have rejected him; for the LORD sees not as man sees; man looks on the outward appearance, but the LORD looks on the heart." And so it was. Jesse proceeded to call each of his sons, one by one, until seven of his excellent sons had passed by the prophet Samuel, but, much to his frustration, Samuel was only able to conclude, "The LORD has not chosen these."

And then the situation changed. After Samuel had seen all the others, Jesse sheepishly admitted to Samuel that he had one last son: "There remains yet David, the youngest, but behold, he is keeping the sheep." Now, as most know, herding sheep was a most detestable task. Samuel said to Jesse, " 'Send and fetch him; for we will not sit down till he comes here.' And Jesse sent, and brought David in. Now David was ruddy, and had beautiful eyes, and was handsome. [These attributes reflected David's interior life.] And the LORD said, 'Arise, anoint him; for this is he.' Then Samuel took the horn of oil and anointed David amid his brothers; and the Spirit of the LORD came mightily upon David from that day forward."

About the only thing that counts with people today are outward appearances: how much money they have, how successful they are, their athletic ability; their entire existence is evaluated by how beautiful their bodies are and how attractive their faces. Not so with the Lord, for He says to His prophet, "Do not look on his appearance or on the height of his stature ... for the LORD sees not as man sees; man looks on the outward appearance, but the LORD looks on the heart."

As mentors, we must see in the same manner as the Lord does. If we are to offer ourselves in service to young people, we must possess the same ability to look into the heart of any and every boy and see the good that is always present. Every person, every boy, is wonderfully made—unique and unrepeatable. Yet, as has been said, our young men and boys have been so polluted by the culture and broken by the failure of family and community that they rarely see anything authentically good in themselves.

Ruminate on the Scripture passage.

Is it not interesting to note, since many men are neglected or abandoned by their fathers, or at least may feel that way, that we find David shepherding sheep? The shepherd was a rejected soul, lacking in honor, prestige, and respect.

Had David's father, Jesse, sent the boy away, essentially abandoning him? We can conclude that David, spending his entire day, if not weeks or months, with sheep, lacked precious time with his father and even with his older brothers. In the story of David, we see the sorrowful situation of a boy who was neglected, if not rejected, by his father and sent away to do work that nobody else was willing to do. Note that he was not completely sent away, as he was still within the household of Jesse, but just somehow overlooked. With no one to lavish time and effort upon him, what would become of David? Put yourself in David's sandals: the realization that he was the youngest and the least likely to be afforded his father's love was certainly a crushing blow. We might easily conclude that because of this, his father had wounded David.

Likewise in the modern world, so many of our young people face the same plight as the result of divorce, drug or alcohol abuse, Internet pornography, illicit sexual activity, or, worse, outright emotional neglect. Even boys or young men who have the advantage of having a father who is present often want or need more from him. This may not be anyone's fault, but it is certainly the destructive circumstance of our modern culture. Many, if not most, of our young men find themselves in the same position as David. David is an intriguing character, and we will examine his life more closely later.

At the very core of human existence is an essential requirement to be validated, given "permission" of sorts, to enjoy existence and thrive on the planet. This cannot be overly stressed. A boy who has not been validated by the most powerful person in his life, his father, will ache to fill a gnawing emptiness or an uncertainty in his heart. More than likely, he will never be cognizant that this emptiness is present, but most of his effort, most of his struggle, will be to discover and receive this validation; and most of the places he looks for it will not be powerful enough to deliver him from this dark existence — or may even drive him to despair.

We could offer several studies reinforcing this truth, but consider a more unique source. In one of the few times God the Father speaks in the New Testament, we hear an essential affirmation in the life of Jesus Christ, the beloved Son of the Father. The Scripture relates, "And when Jesus was baptized, he went up immediately from the water, and behold, the heavens were opened and he saw the Spirit of God descending like a dove, and alighting on him; and lo, a voice from heaven, saying, 'This is my beloved Son, with whom I am well pleased'" (Matt. 3:16–17). Now, if this affirmation from the mouth of the Almighty Father was essential even for the Incarnate Word, the Divine Savior, the essential nature of a father's affirmation in the life of a boy is even clearer.

There is more.

St. Peter reinforces the importance of the Father's statement as he elaborates: "For when he received honor and glory from God the Father and the voice was borne to him by the Majestic

Glory, 'This is my beloved Son, with whom I am well pleased,' we heard this voice borne from heaven, for we were with him on the holy mountain" (2 Pet. 1:17–18). We can see that within this affirmation is contained the bestowal of honor and glory by the Father (the Majestic Glory) upon the psyche of His Son.

For earthly fathers, this is not easy to do. As fathers and mentors, we must — absolutely and without question — validate our sons or disciples. This is not accomplished in a moment or in a single encounter. Because of past wounds and a culture that has convinced them otherwise, boys and young men must be *convinced* of their goodness and worth. This may take much time and effort to accomplish properly.

Many have expounded on this concept, so vital to human beings. Holocaust survivor and psychologist Dr. Conrad Baars (1919–1981) had great insights and a profoundly deep understanding of this phenomenon. He masterfully wrote:

> The "other" who wills his awareness of me opens his consciousness to my being, and comes to know, that is, possess my goodness. His evident finding delight in my goodness will be perceived by me. I am revealed to myself as good. I have received from the other what I am. I am no longer alone. I have been linked to another human being in this process of affirmation; not by communication of what I have, but by the revelation, the communion of what I am. In friendship the greatest gift my friend can give me is himself. In affirmation, *I receive an even greater gift: myself.*[36]

---

[36] Conrad Baars, *Born Only Once: The Miracle of Affirmation* (Quincy, IL: Franciscan Herald Press, 1975), 28, my emphasis.

We know that, by definition, love is "giving oneself to the other." As Dr. Baars wisely explains, when we love a friend, we give ourselves to him with a focus on his welfare. Much more significantly and much more remarkably, however, when we affirm another, we give the gift of the person to himself!

From this one excerpt from Dr. Baars's work, we can see the great power that you hold in a mentoring relationship. The only prerequisite is that your disciple respect you. If you are to convince your disciple of his goodness, you must be held in great esteem and even revered. Validation is more effective and complete if your disciple holds a reverential "fear" of you. If you are powerful enough to invalidate your disciple, your validation will mean something to him. With full integrity (i.e., do not say it if you do not believe it), you look into the heart of your disciple and, as Dr. Baars says above, not only give yourself to him but affirm him to the point of giving him the gift of himself.

You are familiar with this: when a father, a grandfather, an older brother, a teacher, a priest, or whoever holds authority profoundly affirms the good in a person, it can change that person forever. When this is accomplished, a disciple who asks himself, "Am I worthy? Have I value?" will now know that someone significant truly believes in him, which will enable him to answer affirmatively, "It is good that I exist." The result is staggering.

Before he was elected supreme pontiff, Joseph Cardinal Ratzinger saw the same need in humanity: "Something strange happens here.... How does one go about affirming, assenting to, one's [self]? The answer may perhaps be unexpected: we cannot do so by our own efforts alone. Of ourselves, we cannot come to terms with ourselves. Our 'I' becomes acceptable to us only if it has first become acceptable to another 'I'. We can love ourselves only if we have first been loved by someone else." He then reminds us that physical life is not enough and concludes, "It is only when life has been accepted and is perceived as accepted that it becomes also acceptable. Man is that strange creature that needs not just physical birth but also appreciation if he is to subsist.... If an individual is to accept himself, someone must say to him: 'It is good that you exist' — must say it, not with words, but with that act of the entire being that we call love."[37]

Continuing to drive this most important point home, we see the same circumstance in the teaching of St. Thérèse of Lisieux, who described this affirmation as an "act of mirroring." Simply described, a young person may not realize his authentic goodness or his potential until he looks into your face as in a mirror and sees his goodness in the admiration you hold for him. In this act of admiration, you communicate to your disciple his goodness, and hence, he learns that there may be more to him than he originally thought. This is a wonderful gift for a young person.

Swiss priest and theologian Hans Urs von Balthasar also saw this necessity. "Man sustains himself — indeed, he first comes to himself — in an encounter. When one man meets another face-to-face, truth comes to pass; the depths of human existence comes to light spontaneously, in freedom and grace.... The two [become] joined in a truth that transcends their finitude."[38]

We see this yet again in the wisdom of Pope St. John Paul the Great: "Man cannot live without love. He remains a being that is incomprehensible for himself, and his life is senseless, if love

[37] Joseph Cardinal Ratzinger, *Principles of Catholic Theology: Building Stones for a Fundamental Theology* (San Francisco: Ignatius Press, 1987), 79–80.

[38] Hans Urs von Balthasar, *Love Alone Is Credible* (San Francisco: Ignatius Press, 2004), 43–44.

is not revealed to him, if he does not encounter love, if he does not experience it and make it his own, if he does not participate intimately in it."[39] Be assured, the saint is not speaking here of spousal love, for, if such an affirmation does not happen in the earlier years of a man's life, he will never be able to recognize it in his spouse, or worse, he may never have the ability to return love selflessly to his wife or his children.

The truth of what is written here cannot be stressed urgently enough. Recently, I had the privilege of talking with a soldier of the United States military. He had a very difficult childhood that left him lost and existentially afraid. Even though he sought to talk with me, a Catholic priest, he declared himself to be an atheist. During our long and thoughtful conversation, the young man related the destructive nature of his relationship with his mother. "She told me that I am no good," he admitted sadly. "She told me that I will never be a good man or amount to anything." And, in that instant, he turned to me with an expression of desperation; his eyes communicated a worried and sorrowful fear that it might be true. He stared hard into my face as he studied my reaction. He was looking for someone, anyone, to tell him this was not true.

Boys (and girls) who grow to adulthood never having been validated by "another" truly live a desperate life. The deficit easily brings about promiscuous sex, drug abuse, identity confusion, disillusionment, narcissism, anger, and, of course, despair. A person who has not been validated will be unable to give or to receive love because his primary question — "Is it good that I

[39] John Paul II, encyclical letter *Redemptor Hominis* (March 4, 1979), no. 10.

exist?"—which can be answered only by "the other," will never have been answered. For him, his own love is meaningless; and love given to him can never be received.

To be sure, affirmation does not come so much in the spoken word. A man cannot approach his disciple and simply say, "I affirm you." A disciple needs years of constant and stable affirmation, most of it nonverbal: a pat on the back, a smile when something good is accomplished, shared joy in the completion of a goal, no possibility of rejection in the face of failure, helping a disciple learn skills, and communicating that he has "what it takes," your presence at important events, and faithful, unreserved investment.

Returning to the story of young David: We are aware that David did not become a great man and a leader of his people on his own. As a man, he also shared the need of essential validation, but in his case, he received it directly from God. Although David was neglected by his earthly father, God the Father intervened and accomplished the task Himself. David spent most of his youth tending sheep in the wilderness. It was there, as with many of our saints, that he encountered God—amidst the beauty and solace of God's creation. He spent this time in contemplation and prayer, dwelling alone with his Heavenly Father. David's intuitive openness to the Divine enabled him to be fathered and validated by Israel's God. In Psalm 73, David revealed his intimate relationship with his Heavenly Father: "Nevertheless, I am continually with thee; / thou dost hold my right hand. / Thou dost guide me with thy counsel, / and afterward thou wilt receive me to glory. Whom have I in heaven but thee?" (vv. 23–25). If we do not receive this affirmation from our earthly fathers (as God intended), or from a generous mentor, we can still receive it from our Heavenly Father—although not receiving the affirmation from our natural father makes receiving it from our Heavenly Father even more difficult.

Self-Confidence

Telling a person that he must "believe in himself" has lost its effectiveness and is viewed by most young people today as a worthless cliché. Young people certainly have lost a sense of their dignity and sacredness. Although young people may dismiss this "cliché," they have not moved beyond the need to know that they are created by God as unique and unrepeatable individuals. A man who does not "believe in himself," by which we mean "believe in his innate goodness" — that he has unlimited potential and an ultimate destiny — is at a distinct disadvantage.

I have spent a good amount of time detailing the effect our disordered culture has had upon our young people. But the most grievous effect has been the impoverished regard young people have for themselves. When a person does not believe in himself, he cannot dream, he cannot resist temptation, his relationships suffer, and he settles for mediocrity. St. Leo the Great stressed this emphatically when he proclaimed, "O Christian, remember your dignity and, now that you share in God's own nature, do not return to your former base condition by sinning."[40] By this, the saint means that, following Baptism, when we are gloriously adopted as sons and daughters of our Almighty Father, we must always conduct ourselves as men destined for glory. Simply remembering who we are has an immense capacity to empower us to overcome weakness and strive for greatness.

---

[40] St. Leo the Great, *Sermo 22 in nat. Dom.*; quoted in the *Catechism of the Catholic Church*, no. 1691.

My first encounter with a young man addicted to drugs taught me the significance of self-belief. Michael had been beaten, arrested, and abandoned by family and friends, and had attempted suicide several times. When I met him, I asked nothing of him; we only spent time together. After all, I was new to the priesthood, and aside from praying for him, I honestly had no idea how to help the young man.

Then, one beautiful October day, sitting at the edge of a lake, he looked at me—unashamed of the tears he was unable to suppress—and asked me why "someone as important" as I, "with so many responsibilities," cared about him. He accused himself of horrible crimes, condemned himself without restraint, and described himself in a most horrific manner. He struggled to find words ugly enough to express his self-hatred. He had long ago abandoned any belief in his goodness before God or man. In his view, he was worthless, and his dark destiny was assured.

When he was finished, he sat and stared intently into my face. He longed to know that all he had told me was not true. He needed someone who was honest and whom he respected to tell him that he was wrong. Finding words powerful enough was not easy, but I started by shaking my head and telling him how wrong he was, that he had fallen for the lies that plague all mankind. And I began to teach him—or more accurately, tried to convince him—that he was loved.

Why do so many young people use drugs, mutilate themselves with tattoos and piercings, engage in illicit sexual activity, and settle for wretched mediocrity? The causes are many, but at the core, young people do not believe in their goodness, their potential, their true purpose, and their greatness of soul. Stand squarely before a young man and look him in the eye. You know what will follow: he will look away, unable to withstand a face-to-face encounter. Why? Even though he may be indignant and exhibit outward signs of irritation by your posture, he fears he will be exposed as a fraud. He simply does not believe in himself and is likely to be struggling with feelings of inadequacy. To push this to its limit, hand a tool to a young man on a work site. Rarely, with some exceptions, will he know how to use the tool properly. He knows this. He will stand before you in self-condemnation as he struggles with feelings of inadequacy.

The most common obstacle to personal growth is this radical disbelief in one's goodness and worth. Where do young men receive intentional and authentic affirmation today? Where are their fathers? Where are their uncles, their male teachers, and their mentors? A mentor can affirm his disciple by mirroring back to him his own goodness, inestimable worth, and true potential. Of course, this is not easy to do when dealing with a young man whose interior development has been neglected for many years and who has been taught that men (especially white men) are responsible for the many evils plaguing society. At this point, a mentor's intervention may be somewhat limited in its effectiveness, as there is so much for him to overcome. If essential affirmation did not happen in childhood, it is nearly impossible for a person to recover or to "heal" from this loss. You must faithfully do what you can. The more your disciple believes in you, the more powerful and effective your intervention will be.

Deliberateness

Deliberateness is the key to male development and absolutely makes the man. The most successful men with whom I have had the privilege to work understood and embraced the discipline of deliberateness. It is what made them successful! Deliberateness safeguards the goals and direction of a young man's life. So often, we encounter young men who truly want to grow and maximize their potential but are waylaid by a myriad of senseless activities and distractions. As has been said, if an activity is too challenging, not "fun," or not sensually profitable, young people lose interest rather quickly. Deliberateness is the constant in the equation that keeps exceptional men focused and on track.

A young man should be encouraged to contemplate — in detail — the type of man he wishes to become. His discernment must be precise and detailed. He should envision the virtues, qualities, and characteristics that are most important to him. He might be asked how he would like to see himself in five, ten, or twenty years. The mentor must also be aware that, more than likely, he will want to become a man like you, which is another reason to be the best man you can be.

When his vision is clear, he must be challenged to live deliberately. Thus, during every moment of his day, he asks himself, "Am I being deliberate in this moment? Will the activity that I am engaged in help me to become the man I envision?" If he has thirty minutes free, deliberateness directs him to use his time wisely. All daily, weekly, and monthly activities ought to pass the litmus test of deliberateness. Consequently, when a young man comes home from work, he can waste time watching television, reading about other people's lives on social media, or playing video games. Alternatively, he might read the biography of a great man, exercise, volunteer, learn a skill, go to Mass, earn a master's degree — the possibilities are limitless. He may need to be encouraged, but success is guaranteed by his ability to practice deliberateness.

I had the pleasure to work with an impressive group of young men in my parish. They understood and eagerly embraced the concept of deliberateness, but one of their number "fell in love" while in high school. He withdrew from his peers and began spending much time with his new girlfriend—an admittedly enjoyable pursuit. Yet this was contrary to what I had taught him. I had urged the young men not to date until age twenty-one, reminding them that they had little to offer a woman before they had completed the work of becoming a man. In this case, the young man's absence was to his own detriment. He forfeited much growth by abandoning the intentional work of formation. Years later and with great maturity, he admitted to me that he would have been better off sticking to the program and spending those years intentionally working on becoming a better man.

A father told a similar story of his son, who was impressive by all measures. He interacted with a small "fraternity" of his peers to the great benefit of all: they traveled, studied, and experienced many things together, even teaching themselves blacksmithing. Then he, too, "fell in love" and abandoned his friends and their intentional work. His father noticed him "sitting on the stairs" having long talks with his girlfriend or hanging out at the shopping mall with her. Finally, his father told him that he did not like what his son was becoming and shared his concern that his son's girlfriend was "feminizing" him. He challenged his son to return to his former manner of life, and his son did so. In other words, his father urged him to be intentional in his growth.

Deliberateness also assures the mentor that the disciple is not developing a debilitating dependence. Deliberateness is born in initiative. If a disciple is not building on your combined effort and excelling in areas even beyond your work together, he has not yet taken personal responsibility for his own growth and his future. It is a matter of challenging him to take the initiative and to live intentionally.

Challenge

There is a bit of an art to challenging a young man. If the mentor is to be of any worth to his disciple, he must, sometimes after much experience, extend an occasional challenge to his disciple. Before he does so, he must truly know and understand his disciple. Once again, we are in the realm of something that is quite countercultural. The culture tells us to accept a person "where he is." If, by this maxim, we mean to understand and know an individual, especially in his strengths and weaknesses, the maxim has merit.

But if we mean to accept weaknesses and shortcomings as normative without any challenge to grow, the maxim is despicable. The relationship between a mentor and his disciple is worthless if he cannot extend challenges to the betterment of his disciple. This often requires courage on the part of the mentor, who must know when to push and when to rest, and on the part of the disciple, who must trust his mentor and be docile to his direction.

A seminarian once sat before me in a private conference. I had quickly assessed that he was a man of great potential and was squandering much of his opportunities for leadership and other worthwhile contributions because of his lack of self-confidence. Assessing that the time had arrived, I challenged him thus: "Andrew, do you realize that you are an alpha male?" Naturally, this warranted his attention, and he looked at me intently and asked, "What do you mean?" I was then able to communicate to him that he had reserves of potential. I told him that he was a natural-born leader who could bring about great change in the world and that other men would be naturally drawn to him and would eagerly submit to his leadership. Further, I told him that men would see him as the standard by which to measure themselves. I assured him that he had a sharp intellect that was woefully underdeveloped. I concluded that he had, it seemed to me, an obligation to develop these skills and put them to use for the good of those around him. His response astonished me. After a short period of silence and suppressed sobs, he said to me, "Six years of seminary formation, and nobody has ever said that to me." I told him that that was unfortunate. He took the lead from there, pushing himself with new vigor and manly resolve. He was a joy to watch.

More than anything else, a disciple will appreciate his mentor's ability and willingness to challenge. If done in a clumsy manner, challenging a disciple has the potential to destroy the relationship; on the other hand, the reward for a properly leveled challenge is great.

The soft and accepting type will cringe at the necessity of the challenge. If there is anything in this book that might warrant the accusation of machismo-ism, this may very well be it. Repeatedly, I have met with young men and have issued preliminary challenges: stop wasting time on video games, Netflix, and social media; tackle the pornography problem; read; exercise; work hard. You would think they would never return, but they always do.

Before a challenge is issued, a mentor must wholly and thoroughly know his disciple. This will require a profound and trusting relationship. A mentor must be prudent to extend challenges worthy of his disciple, challenges that are realizable and will not inadvertently crush him. Hopefully, all of us have had the experience of knowing a man who issued an appropriate challenge to us and changed the very course of our lives.

Power

One of the most satisfying aspects of being a male is the privilege of managing the power that comes with being a man. As a young man, I felt it in my bones: following a growth surge, I suddenly found myself the protector, the defender, and, if I was deemed worthy, someone whom others could rely on with confidence. I truly believe and eagerly accept that a man, by nature, is granted a certain amount of raw power. If that power is properly fostered, tempered in self-confidence and self-mastery, a man will see the benefits of his power grow exponentially. Add youth, strength, personality, and virility to power, and the possibilities become limitless. Keep in mind that the power that nature provides to men must be used with prudence. Along with power, men are granted freedom to choose precisely how they will use that power: for good or for evil.

Admittedly, many today are utterly and completely terrified by the thought of anyone wielding power. A friend recently applied for a rather high post with the federal government. When he did not make the final cut, someone on the inside, who desperately wanted to hire him, asked him to resubmit his application. To make his application more competitive, he was encouraged to list his disabilities: his adult ADHD, his heart problems, and his obesity. These, it was thought, would give him an advantage in the hiring process. Notwithstanding the good intentions of federal bureaucrats to give everyone an equal opportunity for employment, one must, in a politically incorrect vein, be some-what perplexed at the thought of a system that penalizes the strong among us.

I value situations in which I was overlooked because of my shortcomings, as the experiences pushed me to work harder. Likewise, when psychologists or educators seek to address the phenomenon of bullying in our schools, the focus is typically placed on coping skills, reporting, and victim assistance. Again, there is no mention of the perpetrator, who obviously must be challenged to learn appropriate conduct. It is almost as if we, collectively, are afraid of the bully. Perhaps this is terrible to write and more difficult to read, but these examples are indicative of our society's contemporary mind-set. Power and powerful people are not considered an asset in our politically correct universe.

Of course, men must realize the proper use of their power. Pope Benedict provided a profound catechetical reflection on the legitimate use of power. "Human logic," he told us, "often seeks self-fulfillment in power, in domination, in forceful means." He went on to say that man, even now, seeks to build the Tower of Babel using his own human power in a misdirected effort to reach the heights of God by himself, to be like God but apart from God. He continued, "The Incarnation and the Cross remind us that complete fulfillment lies in conforming our human will to the will of the Father, in emptying ourselves of our selfishness, to fill ourselves with God's love, with his charity, and thereby become capable of truly loving others." And he goes further: "If [man] wanted to imitate God, this was not a bad thing, but he had the wrong idea of God. God is not someone who only wants greatness. God is love, which was already given in the Trinity and was then given in the Creation. Imitating God means coming out of oneself, giving oneself in love."[41]

"Behold the man!" (John 19:5). Every man is given the freedom and the ability to choose. Each man must decide whether he will stand with Jesus and use the power with which he has been entrusted for the good of others, giving himself in love. This is the legitimate use of power, and it can resonate deeply in the heart of young men.

Will a man use his power in a generative fashion: serving, protecting, encouraging, and building the Kingdom? Will he use

[41] Benedict XVI, General Audience, June 27, 2012.

his power to defend justice and the poor? Will he place his power and might at the service and advantage of others, including his wife, children, coworkers, and neighbors? Will he use his power nobly and resist twisting situations to his own advantage and reveling in a narcissistic lifestyle?

This does not imply, in any sense, that a man must be soft, emotional, or weak. You have heard the common objection: "But we are Christian; we are not to give offense! Jesus said, 'If anyone strikes you on one cheek, turn to him the other also.'"

Is that what Jesus said?

Look at the statement in context: "Do not resist one who is evil. But if any one strikes you on the right cheek, turn to him the other also; and if anyone would sue you and take your coat, let him have your cloak as well; and if any one forces you to go one mile, go with him two miles" (Matt. 5:39–41). Jesus uses "turn the other cheek" to explain that if you are generous to a person and he takes advantage of you, you should be unreservedly quick to be generous again. This, it is hoped, will win your brother to God. Examine Jesus: "When he had said this, one of the officers standing by struck Jesus with his hand, saying 'Is that how you answer the high priest?' Jesus answered him, 'If I have spoken wrongly, bear witness to the wrong, but if I have spoken rightly, why do you strike me?'" (John 18:22–23). Jesus does not turn the other cheek, inviting abuse; He defends the truth that He has spoken. Are we not to do the same?

Critics will not understand or accept any of this. They will make insolent accusations that we believe men should stand shirtless under the moon and pound their chest and howl like the devil. Next will follow more accusations of machismo-ism. Because they are not men, or do not know how to act like men, they will never see the good in power, nor will they feel the responsibility to use it properly. The concept is not that difficult. Young men know they possess power (as do young women, but in a much different manner); we seek only to acknowledge their power as good and encourage them to use it wisely.

More than 150 years ago, a bloody battle waged in the small village of Gettysburg, Pennsylvania. The armies of General Meade and General Lee slammed into each other with some of the most violent fighting of the Civil War. On the third day of the battle, General Lee had his greatest opportunity for success: he had pushed his men far into the Northern states, knowing that a victory in Pennsylvania would demoralize the Northern army as well as the nation's citizenry and guarantee European support of the Southern cause. At the height of the third day of the battle, Union General Winfield Hancock realized that the Union army had a break in their lines that could be easily exploited by General James Longstreet. Hancock needed ten valuable minutes to bring up reinforcements from the Union rear. Assessing the dangerous situation, he commanded the First Minnesota Regiment to charge forward and fill the gap. But the men of the First Minnesota had made an assessment of their own: if they did what General Hancock had commanded them to do, they would likely die.

There was no hesitation. They courageously did what they were commanded. They fought to their death. They preserved the Union lines and saved the Union Army. They preserved the Union itself and helped free the slaves. A surviving member of the First Minnesota Regiment later wrote, "Of the two hundred and sixty-two men who made the charge, two hundred and fifteen lay dead upon the field, struck down by Rebel bullets; forty-seven men were still in line, and not a man deserted."

These men died for people yet unborn, you and me, in a determined, selfless manner. Of course, they thought of home and family as they were dying on the battlefield, but the thought of future generations living free in a blessed republic marked their sacrifice. This is manly power fortified in selfless love.

Man was created for greatness and for power. He should stop turning pale and trembling at the thought of standing strong and using the power with which he has been endowed for the cause of justice, goodness, and right—always guided by virtues in imitation of Jesus Christ and following the way He conducted Himself as a man.

Much is said about Jesus, and many claim Him as the icon representing their own agenda. This much we know about Jesus: He is the King of the universe, and by His power He holds all things together (Col. 1:17). Nevertheless, when He made His triumphal entry into Jerusalem, "they brought an ass and a colt, and put their garments on them, and he sat thereon" (Matt. 21:7). He had no need for pretension or posturing; He had no need to threaten or to instill fear; He sat humbly on the back of a colt and "took possession" of His Kingdom.

All of this can motivate a young man, and if we trust him, he will be of great advantage to our communities. We have only to teach him this truth: the ultimate power is in the ability to love deeply. So let us teach him to love well and to be truly powerful.

Teaching the Virtues

Most boys and young men deeply desire to excel and to be the best men they can be, but most are also at a loss as to how to proceed. An earnest and sincere disciple who is determined to excel will often ask, "What am I to do?" or "How do I become a good, self-mastered man?" A man in his twenties who is flailing in an ocean of emotivism, nihilism, and confusion is extremely eager for answers and direction. Having been raised in a world without legitimate concern for the development of men, he can only react instinctively: his heart tells him there is more, but his experience tells him nothing. Because I have made mentoring a focus of my ministry, I have had a good number of boys and young men ask me, "How do I become a good man? What must I do?" Each time, I am astonished that a young man has the tenacity and the gumption to approach me with such a question.

Once again, we turn to the ancient wisdom of the Church for a solution. She offers a program of sorts to help young people negotiate life and seize the opportunity for formative growth. Any attempt at mentoring must include at least an introduction to the virtues.

The *Catechism of the Catholic Church* (CCC) offers a useful definition of the virtues: "Human virtues are firm attitudes, stable dispositions, habitual perfections of intellect and will that govern our actions, order our passions, and guide our conduct according to reason and faith" (1804). To understand the concept of disposition or habit, consider vice, virtue's opposite. Say a man, working for a store owner, is tempted to steal a little money from a safe in the back of the store. The first time he gives in to this temptation, he may enjoy the payoff, but he will have to live with the rumblings of his conscience. The next time he is tempted, he is more comfortable with the idea, less afraid of being caught, and more enticed by the reward. His wicked success leads him to more and more inappropriate behavior. Soon, he does not even think about his action, and when the opportunity presents itself, he acts quickly and efficiently and seems to profit from his habit. The evil act is accomplished with ease and without forethought. St. Thomas Aquinas would consider this a bad disposition, which leads us to actions not in accord with our dignity and will not assist us in achieving perfection and personal well-being.

Virtue, by contrast, does the opposite. As the *Catechism* teaches, virtues are dispositions or habitual perfections that govern our actions, enabling us to live not by our base passions but according to "reason and faith." Virtues are essentially good habits that are accomplished to our good and appropriate end. A virtue is not present until an act is accomplished with ease.

The Church offers four virtues that are indispensable to a Christian man: prudence, justice, fortitude, and temperance. The importance of these virtues is made manifest by the fact the Church has named them cardinal, or "hinge," virtues.

Prudence, for example, "is the virtue that disposes practical reason to discern our true good" (CCC 1806). Practically speaking, I often tell troubled boys or young men to think, think, and think again, before acting in a situation. Boys are frequently accused of reckless and dangerous behavior. Often a boy's recklessness is due more to a lack of prudence than to a desire to cause harm. To be prudent, a man must allow his conscience or right reason to be his guide and to direct his action, especially in the face of a moral question. The virtue of prudence has the capacity to correct stupid or immoral behavior and direct a man to better alternatives. In the secular realm, prudence can be mistaken for timidity or fearfulness, but consistently acting well is a mark of a true and dependable man.

Justice "is the moral virtue that consists in the constant and firm will to give their due to God and neighbor" (CCC 1807). Justice demands that we respect the rights and dignity of our neighbor and live in harmony with him and with God. Justice is not egalitarianism or tolerance; it is uprightness of conduct toward our neighbor. A lazy man who does not earn his pay is stealing from his employer and is not acting justly. A boy who physically attacks another because of his race or his effeminate behavior is acting unjustly. A man who has promiscuous sexual relations, taking advantage of another, is acting without justice toward his neighbor. By contrast, a man who puts in a full day's work, protects the reputation of his girlfriend, treats another man (whatever his race) with respect, or pays his employees a fair wage acts justly.

Fortitude "is the moral virtue that ensures firmness in difficulties and constancy in the pursuit of the good" (CCC 1808). Fortitude is the training in strength that is needed to endure trials and overcome moral difficulties. A high school boy was invited to a party. At sixteen years of age, he was excited to be invited and saw this as a first step into the world of his peers. When he arrived at the party, all seemed well enough, but as he made his way to the back of the house, he noticed a large display of drugs and alcohol. He easily could have overlooked the display or even participated in the illicit recreation. But he gathered himself, took a deep breath, thanked the host of the party for his invitation, and walked out the front door. He knew this would open him to ridicule and harassment by his peers, as the pressure to conform was enormous. Yet he remained faithful to his convictions and left. To his great surprise, he was followed by a good number of his peers — boys looking for a leader who was unafraid to do what was right. This is fortitude in action.

Temperance "is the moral virtue that moderates the attraction of pleasures and provides balance in the use of created goods" (CCC 1809). Often misunderstood to be the virtue of teetotaling grandmothers, temperance is all about self-mastery; it is a healthy discretion, a moderation or sobriety of living. An animal has no discretion and will live entirely within the dictates of its passions or desires. Man, however, has the use of reason and can discern the value in conforming his will to his intellect. In his

Letter to the Romans, St. Paul describes the fate of men who failed to live by reason: "They became futile in their thinking and their senseless minds were darkened. Claiming to be wise, they became fools.... Therefore God gave them up in the lusts of their hearts to impurity, because they exchanged the truth about God for a lie.... For this reason God gave them up to dishonorable passions" (1:21–26). Reason and restraint did not govern their lives as they should.

The *Catechism* concludes that virtues "make possible ease, self-mastery, and joy in leading a morally good life. The virtuous man is he who freely practices the good" (1804). Thus, a boy who struggles mightily with chastity, putting up a good fight amid temptation, turmoil, and overpowering passion, even if he is successful, is not yet virtuous. He may be heroic, but he is not yet virtuous. The virtuous person experiences an "ease" resulting from self-mastery that leads to a joy of moral living. With virtue, his decision to do good and the requisite follow-through are accomplished almost effortlessly.

Returning to our example of vice given above, when a man feels tempted to steal from his employer but can resist, he will find the next temptation to steal less of a burden. If he can maintain this behavior, then, when the temptation to steal even enters his mind, he will quickly and resolutely dismiss the notion.

How does one acquire virtue?

In two ways.

First, God has the power and the desire to infuse virtues into the heart of man. Prayer, then, is essential to the man who desires to be virtuous. He must turn to God regularly and implore Him for the grace of virtue.

Second, if a man wants to be virtuous, he must simply act virtuously. If he wants to be courageous, he must act courageously.

If he wants to be chaste, he must act chastely. If he wants to be just, he must act justly. The *Catechism* assures us that "the moral virtues are acquired by human effort. They are the fruit and seed of morally good acts" (1804).

Overcoming Mediocrity with Magnanimity

Magnanimity, from the Latin words *magnus* (great) and *animus* (soul) is greatness of soul. Of the countless young men I have had the privilege to encounter, I have yet to find one who did not respond eagerly to the call to be great. Moreover, a disciple who is presented with the challenge of magnanimity will grow in his fondness for his mentor, because he will see that his mentor believes in him and considers him to be worthwhile and capable of living a magnanimous life.

In his book *Created for Greatness: The Power of Magnanimity*, Alexandre Havard makes some important distinctions in our understanding of magnanimity by exploring the teaching of Aristotle. "Aristotelian magnanimity is that of the philosophers who hold the world in contempt the better to affirm man. It is equanimity in the face of the vicissitudes of life, indifference to dishonor (unless deserved), and contempt for the opinion of the multitude." By this, Aristotle means that the magnanimous man "rises above" the distractions, hardships, and difficulties of life and reigns supreme. "Without this awareness of one's dignity and greatness," Havard teaches, "there is no magnanimity and no leadership."[42] In other words, Aristotle considered magnanimity the greatness of man. Rejecting opinion and common fads while negotiating the challenges of life, the magnanimous man

---

[42] Alexandre Havard, *Created for Greatness: The Power of Magnanimity* (New Rochelle, NY: Scepter Press, 2014), 2.

rises above these trivialities to confront the world with poise and composure.

Havard then turns to the true philosopher of virtue, St. Thomas Aquinas, who considers magnanimity somewhat differently:

> For Thomas Aquinas... magnanimity is the insatiable appetite for great things (*extensio animi ad magna*); the magnanimous person is one whose heart is set on conquering the world and achieving personal excellence.... Magnanimity is a longing for greatness—a burning desire, a sacred quest, and aspiration.... Magnanimity is the virtue of aggressiveness; it is ever prepared to attack, to conquer, to act with the impetuosity of a lion.[43]

This does not mean that the magnanimous person walks on the moon or takes up office in the White House. He is the servant among us—someone who uses his power for the good and well-being of others. He overcomes his weaknesses and shortcomings to live greatly among us: assisting the poor, generating good, defending against evil, creating harmony among men, lifting up the lowly, and living in imitation of Jesus Christ.

A favorite story I learned in my youth demonstrates magnanimity impressively. Shortly after the Southern forces were repulsed during Pickett's Charge at the Battle of Gettysburg, General Robert E. Lee mounted his horse and turned south in utter defeat. He knew that the outcome of the war had been decided on that battlefield. As he began to ride south with the burden of the day resting upon him, a wounded Union soldier raised himself up and shouted, "Hurrah for the Union!" This caught the general's attention, and he dismounted. The Union

---

[43] Ibid., 3.

soldier immediately realized the stupidity of his act and thought for certain that the general would pull out his revolver and finish him. But the respected general knelt beside him, shook his hand, and wished him well, hoping he would be able to return soon to his family. Then the general mounted his horse and departed. As the story goes, the Union soldier cried himself to sleep.

Another story is told of General Ulysses Grant during the Battle of Chickamauga. Grant and his entourage were on horseback and moving to another part of the battlefield. As they came upon a bridge, they encountered several Confederate prisoners of war. Union officers barked demeaning commands to the prisoners and cleared the bridge for the Union commander. As Grant's entourage thundered over the bridge, no attention was given to the prisoners. Yet, as the general passed the Confederate soldiers, he tipped his hat to them in a gentlemanly manner. The dejected soldiers never forgot the gesture.

Havard contrasts the teachings of the two great philosophers of magnanimity:

> Aquinas takes up the formulas of Aristotle, but gives them a different meaning. Whereas Aristotle says the magnanimous man considers himself worthy of great things (great honors), Aquinas says the magnanimous man considers himself worthy of *doing* great things, which he aims to accomplish for themselves and their inherent grandeur. At the same time, he finds that, without wanting to, he has merited honor, and now must make good use of it.[44]

---

[44] Ibid., 6.

Magnanimity, then, is born in man's awareness of his dignity and greatness; a realization that he was created unique and that there is no one who will follow him who will be like him. With this frame of mind, he cannot be narcissistic or self-oriented (or pusillanimous) but must always look beyond himself for the good he has yet to accomplish. The action of the magnanimous person is never directed to the accolades or flattery of men. The magnanimous person acts as an agent, a force for good, and an enemy of evil. He is not hobbled by the pettiness of life (emotional injuries, harmless discomforts, personal setbacks, or things such as video games, Netflix, and pornography) but gives himself to action befitting the son of a King.

As for our young men, we can settle on the commonly held maxim "boys will be boys" and let them sink into mediocrity. Or, we can challenge them to strive for greatness. A true mentor will identify mediocrity and help his disciple reject it. Although the mentor should not tell a young person, "You can be anything you want" (because it is simply not true), he must convince his disciple that he can achieve great things. Any one of us has the ability and the power to be someone great and to accomplish great things.

Finally, and most importantly, an effective mentor will be very careful to remind his disciple of the true source of his greatness. Jean Cardinal Daniélou eloquently exhorts men with words of truth that will resonate in the heart of any disciple, correcting our assumption that natural ability outweighs supernatural assistance:

> But the saints are not like that. Humanly speaking they are often cowardly and weak, yet they undertake hard things, superhuman tasks, relying on the power of God.... Heroism shows what man can do; holiness shows what can be done by God.... Christianity does not consist in

the strivings of man after God, but in the power of God, accomplishing in man that which is beyond the power of man; human efforts are merely the response called forth by the divine initiative.[45]

In fact, Father Cajetan Mary da Bergamo gives us a solemn warning to be kept in mind by one accomplishing great things: "But if I am proud, I become like a thief, appropriating to myself that which is not mine, but God's."[46]

Mention must be made of a necessary companion to magnanimity: the virtue of humility. Humility, contrary to much misunderstanding, is defined as the "truth of oneself." Thus, a man can be truly great but must always be grounded in humility. He understands that his greatness and potential—down to the air that he breathes—is a gift from God. Jewish elders often exhorted their sons to carry two pieces of paper in their pockets. On one piece, they were to write, "I am everything" and on the other, "I am nothing." A true and humble person lives within the tension of the two.

Jesus opens His Sermon on the Mount with the exhortation "Blessed are the poor in spirit, for theirs is the kingdom of heaven" (Matt. 5:3). This is not an affirmation of material poverty, as some might think. Poverty is a wretched state to which nobody ought to be subjected.

Jesus speaks of poverty of spirit in much the same way Jewish fathers taught their sons. Jesus is acknowledging that man

[45] Jean Daniélou, *The Lord of History: Reflections on the Inner Meaning of History*, trans. Nigel Abercrombie (London: Longmans, Green, 1958), 115.

[46] Cajetan de Bergamo, *Humility of Heart* (New York: Veritatis Splendor Publications, 2012), 20.

is weak and even prone to evil. A man poor in spirit is aware of his limitations, his struggles with sin, and his nothingness, especially before God.

But in addition to this awareness, he is also aware of his status as a revered son of God — even if he cannot perceive the greatness of his status. Thus, a man poor in spirit lives in complete cognizance of the tension between these two realities.

Fraternity and Friendship

Competition is one of the most intriguing aspects of being male. Women and elites often lament that competition creates brutes and are loath to understand why men profit from male competition. Quite impressively, competition is a remnant of our evolutionary past and may be as old as our DNA. Thousands of years ago, competition was essential for the defense of a tribe or village. Boys and young men would literally run in social packs over the course of their lives for a very specific reason: competition was necessary to identify the future alpha male, who would be responsible for the safety and well-being of the tribe. But competition also identified and organized the power hierarchy that the alpha male would lead: which man had which skill — a necessity for the organization and defense of the community.

That is why, even today, men can engage in brutal competition and immediately thereafter gather around a bar and enjoy each other's company. Following competition, there is mutual respect, admiration, and appreciation for one another. More importantly, following competition, each man knows what the man standing on either side of him can do and knows which man he might rely on in dangerous situations. If a man gives his unreserved best and gives a respectable effort, he will experience no shame within the hierarchy.

Men thrive in these circumstances. Competition offers an honest assessment of an individual and, should he fail to "measure up," he will simply find it necessary to work harder. This is essential. Today, due to misguided egalitarian concerns, boys and men who excel are often scolded and labeled "oppressive" or, in a pejorative manner, "aggressive." They are indoctrinated with the notion that everyone is equal, and everyone has a "right" to engage at every level. Egalitarianism is a fantasy, and men will never be able to accept this artificial social construct.

It might seem a bit odd to begin the section on friendship with competition. But both friendship and competition accomplish the same goal: to make us better men. I once knew a very successful man of Lebanese descent who was the father of two boys. He drilled into his sons a very important principle about friends: "Either you will stop being his friend, or you will become like him." This is a twofold message: if a young man's friend is good, his association will be personally beneficial, and his friend's influence will make him a better man. In this case, if he is not interested in self-improvement, the friendship will terminate.

Alternatively, if his friend lacks good character and is prone to act poorly, the opposite will occur, and the influence upon him will be detrimental. In this case, if he is not interested in being dragged down with the resulting mediocrity, the friendship will terminate. Living by this principle would inoculate many of our boys and young men from influences detrimental to their development.

But this valuable principle also reminds us that friendship is essential in the life of men — especially for continued growth toward excellence. As iron sharpens iron, the Scriptures say, so one man sharpens the life of another (Prov. 27:17). This is not to say a young man should abandon his friend who may need intervention as well as a positive influence in his life, but it presents the case for caution. The troubled boy or young man ought to be given the opportunity, the extended hand of friendship, but if the invitation to positive change is rejected, one would be well advised to move on.

Many, if not most, men lack the opportunity for friendship today. Sadness permeates the soul of a man who does not have the pleasure of a friend or two. Technology and social media have had the unexpected result of isolating most men, and many negotiate life without the benefit of real friendship and camaraderie.

Mention must be made of the perceived social stigma related to male friendship. Many men are often uncomfortable in the presence of other men today and would rather not be accused of an inappropriate or suspicious relationship. After all, we do live in an overly sexualized society.

Few men in our history were as great as St. Augustine, bishop of Hippo, a Roman province in North Africa. In his remarkable autobiography, *The Confessions*, he recalls a friendship he enjoyed in his youth. Following the death of this friend, he openly and without shame lamented,

> I was amazed ... that I could go on living myself when he was dead—I, who had been like another self to him. It was well said that a friend is half one's own soul. I felt that my soul and his had been but one soul in two bodies, and I shrank from life with loathing because I could not bear to be only half alive; and perhaps I was so afraid of death because I did not want the whole of him to die, whom I had loved so dearly.[47]

---

[47] Augustine of Hippo, *The Confessions*, bk. IV, 6–7.

The intensity of this relationship is astonishing. Is it any wonder that some in the contemporary world would use the saint's reflection to accuse him of homosexuality? Regrettably, some have. The homoerotic interpretation of male friendship has driven a wedge between men.

The men with whom I associate know quite well the benefit of friendship and fraternity. How many nights have we spent on a mountain or in a forest, under the stars and before a glowing fire? A modest drink, a cigar in hand, and following the jocularity typical of men, the conversation that often turns to accountability, the future, society, relationships, family, history, religion, and philosophy. The men who run in my circles rarely miss these opportunities. Titles of books are exchanged, philosophical thought is assessed, struggles are discussed, societal ills are rehashed, and individual men are often affirmed. Thoughtful wives will sacrifice a night or two with their husbands, as they know the benefits to be gained by them in such an association.

The presence of a friend can change a man forever. I have always encouraged young men to find others who are better athletes; who are stronger intellectually and more familiar with literature; who are firmer in their moral character; who are more experienced in business, auto mechanics, or hunting; and the like. Associating with men who are better than you will propel you to greater knowledge, a stronger character, and success.

Few of my friends know how miserable I was in my first year in high school. I had attended Catholic schools my entire life and was thrust into the culture of public high school. I was shy, painfully reserved, and failing academically. The thought of walking into the school cafeteria alone to eat lunch sent me into a panic.

To this day, I have no idea why an upperclassman named Byron took an interest in me. Byron enjoyed an extraordinary reputation among teachers, staff, and students. As a high school student, he raised cattle, farmed, and was already involved in the agribusiness world. He was a straight-A student and was eager to graduate and begin college studies.

He took me aside one day and reproached me for my mediocrity and dismal attitude. He insisted that I consider my talents, strengths, assets, and, if you will, "power." He admonished me for not setting goals and dreaming about my future. The very fact that a fine man such as Byron took an interest in me changed the course of my life. He was able to do what teachers and principals had attempted to do with me and failed. Would that every young man had the good fortune to benefit from such a friendship!

The need for male friendship has been a part of Christian experience from the beginning. The second- and third-century Desert Fathers provided practical and decisive advice about friendship. The story is told:

> A brother asked an old man, "How is it that in these days some afflict themselves in their manner of life and do not receive grace as the ancients did?" The old man said to him, "In those days there was charity, and each one caused his neighbor to make progress, but now that charity has grown cold, each one pulls his neighbor back, and that is why we do not receive grace."[48]

Heroic Freedom and Self-Giving

On a beautiful summer day in Wichita, Kansas, a small group of young people put kayaks into the Arkansas River for a day of

---

[48] Benedicta Ward, trans. *The Wisdom of the Desert Fathers* (Oxford, England: SLG Press, 1981), 62.

recreation and adventure. As they negotiated the river, which had flooded the day before, they came upon a small waterfall that proved to be turbulent and hard to negotiate. The kayakers—three young women and two young men—quickly found that they were in very difficult and dangerous circumstances. They were tossed from their kayaks and forced to seek refuge on the shore. One of the young women, however, was unable to break free of the undertow and, growing tired, found herself in peril. A young seminarian in the company immediately and without regarding the danger, reentered the water and went to the aid of the young woman. He removed his life jacket, gave it to her, and helped her break free of the undertow. The young man, now exhausted and unable to fight the current, succumbed to the force of the water and drowned.

Long before this incident, this seminarian, Brian Bergkamp, had embraced a life of selfless giving, as evident in his choice to enter the priesthood. This day, he lived heroic self-giving.[49]

St. John Paul II echoed the ancient wisdom of the Church when he addressed young people in his book *Crossing the Threshold of Hope*:

> Clearly, then, the fundamental problem of youth is profoundly personal. In life, youth is when we come to know ourselves. It is also a time of communion. Young people, whether young men or young women, know they must live for and with others; they know that their life has meaning to the extent that it becomes a free gift for others. Here

[49] Catholic News Service, "Body Found of 24-Year-Old Seminarian Who Drowned," *Catholic Herald*, August 4, 2016, http://catholicherald.co.uk/news/2016/08/04/body-found-of-24-year-old-seminarian-who-drowned/.

is the origin of all vocations — whether to the priesthood or religious life, or to marriage and family.[50]

If there is a teaching that has power to transform a person quickly and entirely, this is the principle.

Self-giving is the single most important antidote to a culture that moves us, intentionally or not, to self-worship and radical selfishness. The more deeply a man can give of himself, the happier and more satisfied he will become. I recall listening to a counselor hosting a call-in radio program. One of his callers, a desperate man in California who had decided to commit suicide, pressed the counselor for a reason not to kill himself. The counselor calmly asked the man to make a promise before he committed suicide. The man agreed. The counselor asked the man to do something for someone who did not have the wherewithal to return the favor to him. The desperate man agreed, and the call ended. I had no doubt that the man would be fine. The counselor had put him in touch with the real meaning and purpose of life. How rapidly men would transform themselves, their families, and our culture if they would eagerly and freely place the "other" before themselves. As St. John Paul II has taught, if a man is to have purpose and meaning in his life, he must live for others.

Of course, we cannot give what we do not possess. If a man has not mastered himself, he will not be capable of self-giving. By living a life formed in the virtues — especially chastity — he will be made capable of self-possession and empowered to live a productive and rewarding life of self-giving. St. Paul wrote to the Christians in Rome, "I appeal to you therefore, brethren, by

---

[50] John Paul II, *Crossing the Threshold of Hope* (New York: Alfred A. Knopf, 1994), 121–122.

the mercies of God, to present your bodies as a living sacrifice, holy and acceptable to God, which is your spiritual worship" (Rom. 12:1). Self-giving is not simply a method of living life; it is at the core of what it means to be human. It has the capacity to make us divine. Jesus modeled this principle when He went to the Cross in order to give everything for the good of others. "Greater love has no man than this, that a man lay down his life for his friends" (John 15:13).

Initiation Rites

Before a man is accepted for priestly formation, he must submit an application, which includes an autobiography. I remember reading an application submitted by a candidate who began his autobiography with the intriguing statement: "I grew up on a mountain in Pennsylvania, and my father was my best friend." The statement caught my attention, and I was not surprised when I met the author of the statement and discovered a young man of unlimited potential. He knew who he was; he was secure in his person; and he was trained and ready for whatever the world would place before him.

Every boy deserves this opportunity, and, surely, a modern version of "male initiation" needs to be rediscovered for this to happen. An initiation rite for young men, present in nearly every culture and age, is necessary for the proper formation of boys.

It is disconcerting when we consider that modern societies have all but abandoned any concept or practice of a rite for male initiation. As a matter of fact, the concept of male initiation is now associated with hazing and violence, and sometimes even has sexual connotations. As a result, it has nearly been completely suppressed. The practice seems to be pointless in a society that no longer intentionally forms boys to be men. Too often, boys are required to negotiate life and growth on their own—a very cruel reality for most boys today.

Karen Franklin, a forensic psychologist, summarized her research relative to this topic in the masterful article "Inside the Mind of People Who Hate Gays."[51] Her research led her to the conclusion that violence against homosexual men and women has little to do with homosexuality and more to do with masculine identity and the "masculine problem."

She sees the problem as rooted in a heterosexism, in which "any male who refuses to accept the dominant culture's assignment of appropriate masculine behavior is labeled early on as a 'sissy' or 'fag' and then subjected to bullying." Quite interestingly, she saw in the men she studied a "commitment to the enforcement of masculine norms [stemming] from the nature of masculinity as an *achieved*, rather than ascribed, status [sic]."

In other words, she claims that boys and men are taught what are alleged to be masculine norms innate in the male community (my interpretation) and are intolerant of deviations from these norms because such deviations allegedly characterize men who lack "what it takes to be a man" and who have not successfully engaged in the work necessary to become a man.

Although she may not intend to reinforce gender norms, Franklin's research completely confirms the philosophy of this book as well as the need for male initiation. The weakness of her conclusions, if there is one, is revealed in her pejorative use of the term "masculine." Like many of her contemporaries, she does not see

---

[51] Karen Franklin, "Inside the Mind of People Who Hate Gays," *Frontline Newsletter*, 2016, https://www.pbs.org/wgbh/pages/frontline/shows/assault/roots/franklin.html.

value in masculinity. As we use the term here, masculinity is not "learned" from society as a personal paradigm; it is innate to the male gender, and, as such, the possibility of eradicating masculine identity from a man is all but impossible. Although Franklin does not offer solutions in her article, teaching boys and young men the appropriate use of their masculine power and acknowledging when they do so by use of an initiation rite, would go a long way toward preventing revolting incidents of brutal male behavior.

Building on these findings, Franklin turns to the phenomenon of group escalation, "in which people engage in more extreme behaviors as part of a crowd than they would if alone." She believes that this phenomenon has been "extensively documented" and proven to be "particularly powerful among teenagers and young adults." Thus, she draws the very interesting conclusion that "violence against homosexuals is an ideal way for men to demonstrate their masculinity to their peers." Rather than violence motivated by hatred, she sees that those "perceived to violate gender norms [the effeminate, the homosexual, the weak] function as an ideal dramatic prop for young men to use in demonstrating their masculinity, garnering social approval, and alleviating boredom." Hopefully, the reader can see that a problem is created when thugs, rather than older and mature men, attempt to define masculinity. Violence used as "an ideal dramatic prop for young men to use in demonstrating their masculinity" can easily and effectively be replaced by a legitimate and effective initiation rite.

Franklin states that masculinity is an "achieved" rather than an "ascribed" behavior. This we know; but who is teaching boys and young men what it means to be masculine? Who is holding them accountable for the proper use of the power young men possess? Who is instructing boys and young men in the virtues—a masculine approach to correct and good behavior?

The fact that, as she explains, incidents of violence are escalated by the presence of a group is revealing. The man who practices violence is, perhaps desperately, attempting to convince himself, with the validation of his peers, that he is a true and authentic man. The fact that a test of masculinity (albeit criminal behavior in this case) occurs within the context of a group indicates the need to *be masculine* and for this to be validated by someone outside himself. Again, this corroborates the need for an appropriate rite for male initiation.

Inviting boys and young men into a healthy and productive masculine culture, a culture with responsibility and appropriate and even sacred responsibilities, would hold extraordinary power for them. A rite of initiation would confirm proper conduct and proper purpose for an authentic and worthy man. The validation that would result from correct behavior would come from a man or a society of men rather than a mob of his similarly misdirected peers. The question of whether a boy has become a man would be conclusively answered for him. There would be no need to demonstrate masculinity in a stupid or ridiculous manner.

There is a need for men to weigh Franklin's conclusions:

In contemporary American society, young people — from the poor to the upper middle classes — are systematically neglected and devalued. Lacking access to meaningful, challenging experiences, and sensing a declining potential for success in today's increasingly service-oriented economy, they are often frustrated, discouraged, and socially alienated. Young white males in particular face the contradiction of being taught to expect hegemonic masculine power while being denied any real access to it. This contradiction fosters "power-seeking, adventurous recreational activities at the expense of others who also lack power within the social order," such as women, racial minorities, and homosexuals. Trapped in a temporal vortex between devalued adolescence and adult male privilege, teenage males are given tacit permission to engage in a certain degree of rowdiness and aggression, under the auspices of "boys will be boys." This is particularly true for young men from more privileged strata ... for whom peer group dynamics and thrill seeking often lead to exaggerated displays of masculinity regarding which society largely looks the other way.[52]

[52] Ibid.

10

DEVELOPMENTAL NECESSITY

Becoming a man is a process—a long process of building and refining; one does not reach true and authentic manhood in a day. We see this in the life of King David, who "grew stronger and stronger" (1 Chron. 11:9) and even in the life of our Lord, who "increased in wisdom and in stature, and in favor with God and man" (Luke 2:52).

The life of King David has much to teach a man. He is a type, or foreshadowing, of the perfect man, Jesus Christ. He is the author of many of the psalms, and, as the king of Israel, he is a beloved son of the Father. One of his contemporaries described him thus: "Behold, I have seen a son of Jesse the Bethlehemite, who is skillful in playing, a man of valor, a man of war, prudent in speech, and a man of good presence; and the LORD is with him" (1 Sam. 16:18). We will use David's example as a template to synthesize all that has been covered in this book.

The Sin of David

Those who are familiar with the story of David might, rightly so, be quick to question the appropriateness of placing him before our youth. David is remembered for a great many things, but he is perhaps most remembered for committing adultery with

Bathsheba, the wife of Uriah the Hittite. That, in itself, is an egregious sin; but many seem to forget that, following his infidelity, he also had her unsuspecting husband murdered on the field of battle—not the type of actions one would expect from a model of virtue and character! Is he an appropriate man to inspire the youth of our day? As counterintuitive as it may be, I answer with absolute certitude: yes, he is. There is much to learn from this incident in the life of the king.

The most appropriate place to begin this reflection is the first chapter of the First Letter of John: "If we say we have no sin, we deceive ourselves" (v. 8). Every man has some past mistake, sin, or crime for which he feels acute guilt and shame. As a member of the human race, there is no escaping the snare of evil or the corruption of sin.

I recently met a Vietnam veteran. Within minutes of meeting me, he began relating the story of his service and the responsibility he had to remove undetonated explosives that threatened a local village. He was pensive as he looked to a distant place and described hiring young boys to scour the environs of the village in search of these explosives. By his action, all the boys were placed in grave danger, and a small number were even killed. The unimaginable regret he carried because of this decision had obviously plagued him for years. It is conceivable that a day did not pass in the forty or more years since his tour of duty that he did not condemn himself.

Premarital sex, acts of adultery, accidental deaths, broken relationships, addictions, wasted time, general immorality ... There is one thing common to all humanity: "If we say we have no sin, we deceive ourselves."

But sin should never be allowed to govern or rule our lives, nor should it define who we are. It is our response to sin that has the capacity to define us and even make us better than we were before. We see this in the life of King David.

His sordid tale begins with a very revelatory observation: "In the spring of the year, the time when kings go forth to battle, David sent Joab, and his servants with him, and all Israel; and they ravaged the Ammonites, and besieged Rabbah. But David remained at Jerusalem" (2 Sam. 11:1). This raises an immediate and unsettling question: If "all of Israel" went out to wage war at the time "when kings go forth to battle," why did David not accompany his men? The possibility is real that David was aware of a beautiful woman who lived in the neighborhood and saw the spring warfare as an opportunity to be alone with her.

The Scripture intensifies in the second verse: "It happened, late one afternoon, when David arose from his couch and was walking upon the roof of the king's house, that he saw from the roof a woman bathing; and the woman was very beautiful" (v. 2).

Of course "it happened" — exactly as David had planned! David orchestrated the entire episode, and his plan came to fruition perfectly. Not long thereafter he "took her; and she came to him, and he lay with her" (v. 4). For emphasis, Scripture never refers to Bathsheba by name, but only as "the wife of Uriah." The sin of adultery was freely committed and not long thereafter, Bathsheba sent David the distressing message "I am with child" (v. 5).

There was no immediate repentance. Our hero, the king, was guided by pride. He was more concerned with not being discovered than he was with correcting his fault. And he complicated the matter greatly by plotting and directing the death of Bathsheba's husband. David was about as guilty as a man can be. He believed himself to have been clever and successful in his attempt to conceal his sin, but no sin is private, not one. The tale concludes with these ominous words: "But the thing that David had done displeased the LORD" (v. 27). It was only a matter of time before David was exposed:

> And the LORD sent Nathan to David. He came to him, and said to him, "There were two men in a certain city, the one rich and the other poor. The rich man had very many flocks and herds; but the poor man had nothing but one little ewe lamb, which he had bought. And he brought it up, and it grew up with him and with his children; it used to eat of his morsel, and drink from his cup, and lie in his bosom, and it was like a daughter to him. Now there came a traveler to the rich man, and he was unwilling to take one of his own flock or herd to prepare for the wayfarer who had come to him, but he took the poor man's lamb, and prepared it for the man who had come to him." Then David's anger was greatly kindled against the man; and he said to Nathan, "As the LORD lives, the man who has done this deserves to die; and he shall restore the lamb fourfold, because he did this thing, and because he had no pity." Nathan said to David, "You are the man." (2 Sam. 12:1–7)

After an appropriate tongue lashing by the angry prophet, David uttered the words necessary for his personal restoration, "I have sinned against the LORD" (2 Sam. 12:13). He admitted his sin before God. Yes, he was exposed, and many would be dubious about his "jailhouse conversion." What choice did David have but to confess his sin before the prophet and before God? But that is the point; most people in very similar circumstances would still refuse to admit their guilt. When Adam sinned against God in the Garden of Eden and his sin was discovered, he did not take responsibility, but blamed another: "The woman whom thou gavest to be with me, she gave me fruit of the tree, and I ate" (Gen. 3:12).

"I have sinned against the Lord." This frank, sobering self-accusation went to the heart of God. David had sinned against the God he loved. His words revealed his heart and his willingness to accept whatever punishment was necessary to be reconciled to God.

Following his grievous fall, David is said to have composed Psalm 51 — a perfect prayer of humility and repentance. "Have mercy on me, O God," he laments. "For I know my transgressions, and my sin is ever before me. Against thee, thee only, have I sinned, and done that which is evil in thy sight, so that thou art justified in thy sentence and blameless in thy judgment" (vv. 1, 3–4).

The point will come in any man's life when he must acknowledge his sin or his failure. He will never feel lonelier than in that moment. And making his repentance before God, he must also make a firm resolution to overcome his faults and begin again. In so doing, his repentance and determination to make things right, as much as possible, will forge a new man.

The best men among us have fallen. Knowing the mercy of God and being remade in humility, they are reborn: the murderer becomes the peacemaker; the thief becomes the generous benefactor; the racist becomes the worthy brother; the adulterer becomes the faithful husband; the drunkard becomes the model of temperance; the liar becomes the trusted man; the betrayer becomes the faithful friend. All that is required is the grace and mercy afforded us by so benevolent a God and a firmness of will to do what is good and right. The Christian God is the God of the second chance, as is obvious in the story of Adam and the consequent story of the Second Adam. No one should begrudge the repentant and humble man.

David the Beloved Son

Before anyone knew the name of Israel's greatest King, David was a poor, ridiculous shepherd boy without any prospect of being anything other than a shepherd. But the day came when David found himself standing in the royal court before Saul, the king of Israel. Saul had a problem: Goliath. All of Israel was afraid of Goliath, including the king. But not David: in his youthfulness, he asked publicly why nobody would "take him out," since he had blasphemed the Lord's chosen.

Why was David even near the battlefield? Scripture tells us that he was sent by his father, Jesse, who seemed to have little or no confidence in him, to do what most would have considered "women's work": Jesse said to David, "Take for your brothers an ephah of this parched grain, and these ten loaves, and carry them quickly to the camp to your brothers; also take these ten cheeses to the commander of their thousand. See how your brothers fare, and bring some token from them" (1 Sam. 17:17–18). Jesse sent David to feed his brothers and bring back word of their welfare.

Even though he may not have intended to do so, Jesse must have hurt David deeply. He inadvertently told his son that "he did not have what it takes" to be a battlefield warrior and fight with his brothers. David would remember the pain of his father's slight for years.

Reflect deeply on this. How many times do fathers, even if inadvertently or unintentionally, wound boys by their actions or words? The same question can be asked of mentors. Too often, we men are not attentive to the needs, desires, and emotional lives of our sons and disciples. A young man's heart has wounds; sometimes deep, painful wounds and nearly always unnecessary wounds.

All men seem to share an unmet need for validation. It is one of our most intense desires. Many will ridicule or mock such a notion — a common response from those who cannot comprehend the heart of a man. It is true: until a young man is validated, he will live with a cruel uncertainty deep within himself. More than anyone else, fathers have been given the power and the sacred task of validating their sons, of convincing their sons that it is good that they exist; that they belong and have a place; that they are loved and are lovable. But along with this power, fathers have also been given the power to invalidate.[53]

Of course, few fathers would intentionally invalidate a son, but many have done so by what they said or did not say, or by what they did or did not do for their sons. By virtue of transference (when a disciple sees in the mentor an image of a father), the mentor may have the power to validate. Others believe that, not having received validation from a biological father, all that is possible is validation from God. God can, and does, validate all men. Yet God uses the good men in our lives to communicate that validation concretely to us.

A disciple who yearns to be told that he "has what it takes" has probably spent a good portion of his life yearning for it.

And quite possibly, he only needs to be told (and, many times, he must also be convinced) that it is good that he exists. If this is all that transpires between a mentor and a disciple, it is enough. Knowing of a mentor's confidence and belief in a disciple can

[53] See John Eldredge, *The Way of the Wild Heart: A Map for the Masculine Journey* (Nashville: Thomas Nelson, 2006).

change everything for a young man. In addition, as mentors, we must also encourage our disciples to trust God and allow Him to be a Father to them. Eventually, we must lead them to have complete confidence in God's presence and believe in God's desire to be a Father who sees and hears them. God yearns to father all of us. With all assurance and truth, men must come to see themselves as true sons of the Father.

David spent years in the wilderness, just as Israel did in the Exodus, learning that God is attentive, merciful, kind, and eager to engage his son. Many times, a man needs only to look back on his life to see that God was always there:

When my soul was embittered,
  when I was pricked in heart,
I was stupid and ignorant,
  I was like a beast toward thee.
Nevertheless I am continually with thee;
  thou dost hold my right hand.
Thou dost guide me with thy counsel,
  and afterward thou wilt receive me to glory.
Whom have I in heaven but thee?
  And there is nothing upon earth that I desire besides thee.
My flesh and my heart may fail,
  but God is the strength of my heart and my portion forever.
For lo, those who are far from thee shall perish;
  thou dost put an end to those who are false to thee.
But for me it is good to be near God;
  I have made the Lord God my refuge,
  that I may tell of all thy works. (Ps. 73:21–28)

Only when we abandon ourselves entirely to God and over-come any and all obstacles to His love will we be admitted to sonship with the Father. Pity the man who denies that God exists! Pity the man whose worries or inhibitions become obstacles to his relationship with God. He will never be drawn outside of himself and into the mystery, excitement, and challenge of a son of God.

Too often, young men fall back, listening to the same stale rhetoric they have been programmed to hear and cannot over-come. It is a challenge common to all men. For some, there are many obstacles: doubt (Am I really acceptable to my Father?), uncertainty (I want to believe, but how can I be sure God loves me?), and fear (Who am I to suppose these great things?). Your disciple must cast these thoughts aside. By your patience, love, and support, he must come to understand that he is the beloved son of the Father!

The Potential of David

We pick up the story of David in the first book of Samuel: "When the words which David spoke were heard, they repeated them before Saul; and he sent for him. And David said to Saul, 'Let no man's heart fail because of him [Goliath]; your servant will go and fight with this Philistine.' And Saul said to David, 'You are not able to go against this Philistine to fight with him; for you are but a youth, and he has been a man of war from his youth'" (1 Sam. 17:31–33). Saul has no faith in David and would fret about the boy's safety rather than confess his confidence in him. He loses a remarkable opportunity to build David up in strength and confidence. David said to Saul, "Your servant used to keep sheep for his father; and when there came a lion, or a bear, and took a lamb from the flock, I went after him and struck him and delivered it out of his mouth; and if he arose against me, I caught him by his beard, and struck him and killed him. Your servant has killed both lions and bears; and this uncircumcised Philistine shall be like one of them, seeing he has defied the armies of the living God" (1 Sam. 17:34–36).

Imagine David in the hills of Judah. Is there any doubt he enjoyed the challenge of wrestling "both lions and bears" and killing them? Read this passage allegorically. Boys have many obstacles and fears to overcome. Youth is a time of preparation and formation. This is a direct challenge for a father or a mentor. David had met many challenges and had tested himself. A mentor must discern whether the disciple is truly prepared for the challenges ahead. As for David, he believed in himself and, more importantly, believed that God was with him and had prepared him not only to fight Goliath but to overcome any future obstacles as well.

Would David have even been aware that the time he spent testing himself in the wilderness would have prepared him for the tasks ahead? Although abandoned by his own father, he was not alone. He spent his youth in the companionship of his Heavenly Father, a Father who had great expectations for His son. By grace, David must have intuited this confidence and intentionally sought to prepare himself for the future. How many of our young men squander this time? How many are deliberate about their future, building a secure foundation in the virtues?

Your disciple may be unaware of his potential and may need to be convinced of it. Your utter confidence in him will give him the courage he needs to live the life God intended him to live. Your confidence will afford him the fortitude to accept challenges, to test himself, to resist peer pressure, and in the confrontation of all things evil, to believe in himself.

How many young men who have the capacity to accomplish great feats and overcome shortcomings and weaknesses shrink before the prospect because they do not believe in their own potential?

I was called to the hospital years ago to visit Adam, a sixteen-year-old who had been diagnosed with leukemia. In his room I found a rather large group of relatives who were filled with fear and anxiety. The situation was awkward, and there was little opportunity for conversation. So I asked Adam if he wanted to celebrate the sacrament of Reconciliation. He agreed, and the room emptied of everyone but the two of us. Following his confession, we discussed his situation, his medical prospects, and his anxiety. I took a crucifix from my pocket and handed it to him. I told him that he was sacramentally prepared to accept whatever might come his way. I told him of the redemptive power of suffering and urged him to unite himself to Christ Crucified, as, indeed, he was now called to an exalted and prized vocation of suffering. He listened intently and was eager to accept the cross.

Then he hesitated for a moment, "Why me? Why has God chosen me for this vocation?" I told him the truth: God had raised him to this point in his life because He believed in him. He had been chosen to accomplish this sacred work for the good of the Kingdom. He clasped the crucifix in his hand with a grim and holy determination.

We visited two more times during the week, but by Friday, he had deteriorated rapidly, overcome by a virus. He had to be taken to intensive care, where he was stripped of everything that might interfere with his treatment. When the nurses attempted to remove the crucifix from his hand, however, even as he was unconscious, his grip on it only tightened. Later that day, his body gave out, and he died a painful death. But even during this crisis, he refused to allow the crucifix to fall from his hand. He died a saint, and his parents were adamant that he be buried with the crucifix secure in his hands.

The Evil One would have all of us doubt our potential to live extraordinary or heroic lives. Boys and young men must be given opportunities to prove themselves even to themselves. As fathers and coaches have told boys for years, "The way you play in practice is the way you will play in the game." Going on a hunting trip, backpacking through Europe, pursuing an academic degree, assuming a leadership position, playing on a sports team, rebuilding an old car—these are all ways in which a boy or a young man comes to realize he has what it takes. Otherwise, he is lost to mediocrity and obscurity.

David the Soldier

The story of David and Goliath has become so familiar to us that it is easy to gloss over the event, paying little or no attention to the timeless truth it teaches. Yet this story is for every man: "Let all the men of war draw near, let them come up. Beat your plowshares into swords and your pruning hooks into spears; let the weak say, 'I am a warrior!'" (Joel 3:9–10).

Let us enjoy the story again:

And there came out from the camp of the Philistines a champion named Goliath, of Gath, whose height was six cubits and a span. He had a helmet of bronze on his head, and he was armed with a coat of mail, and the weight of the coat was five thousand shekels of bronze. And he had greaves of bronze upon his legs, and a javelin of bronze slung between his shoulders. And the shaft of his spear was like a weaver's beam, and his spear's head weighed six hundred shekels of iron; and his shield-bearer went before him. He stood and shouted to the ranks of Israel, "Why have you come out to draw up for battle? Am I not a Philistine, and are you not servants of Saul? Choose a man for yourselves and let him come down to me. If he can fight with me and kill me, then we will be your servants; but if I prevail against him and kill him, then you shall be our servants and serve us." And the Philistine said, "I defy the ranks of Israel this day; give me a man, that we may fight together." When Saul and all Israel heard these words of the Philistine, they were dismayed and greatly afraid.

All the men of Israel, when they saw the man, fled from him, and were much afraid.

And David said, "The LORD who delivered me from the paw of the lion and from the paw of the bear, will deliver me from the hand of this Philistine." And Saul said to David, "Go, and the LORD be with you!" Then Saul clothed David with his armor; he put a helmet of bronze on his head and clothed him with a coat of mail. And David belted on his sword over his armor, and he tried in vain to go, for he was not used to them. Then David said to Saul, "I cannot go with these; for I am not used to them." And David put them off. Then he took his staff in his hand, and chose five smooth stones from the brook, and put them in his shepherd's bag or wallet; his sling was in his hand, and he drew near to the Philistine.

And the Philistine came on and drew near to David, with his shield-bearer in front of him. And when the Philistine looked and saw David he disdained him; for he was but a youth, ruddy and comely in appearance. And the Philistine said to David, "Am I a dog that you come to me with sticks?" And the Philistine cursed David by his gods. The Philistine said to David, "Come to me, and I will give your flesh to the birds of the air and to the beasts of the field." Then David said to the Philistine, "You come to me with a sword and with a spear and with a javelin; but I come to you in the name of the LORD of hosts, the God of the armies of Israel, whom you have defied. This day the LORD will deliver you into my hand, and I will strike you down, and cut off your head and I will give the dead bodies of the host of the Philistines this day to the birds of the air and to the wild beasts of the earth; that all the earth may know that there is a God in Israel, and that all this assembly may know that the LORD saves not with sword and spear; for the battle is the LORD's and he will give you into our hand."

When the Philistine arose and came and drew near to meet David, David ran quickly toward the battle line to meet the Philistine. And David put his hand in his bag and took out a stone, and slung it, and struck the Philistine on his forehead; the stone sank into his forehead, and he fell on his face to the ground. So David prevailed over the Philistine with a sling and with a stone, and struck the Philistine, and killed him; there was no sword in the hand of David. Then David ran and stood over the Philistine and took his sword and drew it out of its sheath, and killed him, and cut off his head with it. When the Philistines saw that their champion was dead, they fled. (1 Sam. 17: 4–11, 24, 37–51)

All the power in the universe resides in God. That is why David says to King Saul regarding the armor with which he had been clad, "I cannot go with these; for I am not used to them," and he put them off. A man given to God must know well that "it is the Lord who grants deliverance!" As men, we often try to save ourselves, even though we repeatedly fail when on our own. David was so confident of God's power that he removed any earthly "instrument" upon which he might be tempted to rely (including himself) and put his fate and future in God as his strength. He took no defensive precautions because God alone was his defense.

This is one of the most prominent themes throughout Sacred Scripture: "For with God nothing will be impossible" (Luke 1:37). We pray every day for peace in the world, and we certainly do not want to see any of our young people taken to war. But be it actual war or spiritual warfare, our young men are capable soldiers. They must learn well, like David, to place their trust and confidence entirely in the Lord. We have heard the phrase uttered by Jesus from the Cross, "My God, my God, why have you forsaken me?" (Matt. 27:46). Far from a prayer of despair, Jesus was praying Psalm 22, which ends, "All the ends of the earth shall remember and turn to the LORD ... for dominion belongs to the LORD, and he rules over the nations" (vv. 27–28).

We must eradicate our erroneous ideas about God. For the past fifty years, we have been taught that God is irrelevant or domesticated, a threat to no one, a God whom nobody fears and, therefore, no man respects. But "the fear of the LORD is the beginning of wisdom, and the knowledge of the Holy One is insight" (Prov. 9:10). Men who believe that God is weak and irrelevant will probably be weak and irrelevant themselves, too soft to make a difference in the world. But as we read in Exodus, "The Lord is a warrior; LORD is his name" (see 15:3).

Where are the men filled with righteous anger and ready to fight for the Lord's cause? This cannot be overlooked or ignored! It is the heritage that falls to men: "The LORD raised up a deliverer for the sons of Israel ... Othniel.... The Spirit of the LORD came upon him ... and he went to war" (Judg. 3:9–10). "But the Spirit of the LORD took possession of Gideon; he sounded the trumpet," and he went to war (Judg. 6:34). "And the Spirit of the LORD came upon Jephthah," and he declared war (Judg. 11:29). And just before he killed Goliath, "the Spirit of the LORD came mightily upon David from that day forward" (1 Sam. 16:13).

This is not to be taken as a sanction for brutish force or unwarranted violence. But our version of Christianity must reconcile with the tremendous vision of our Warrior-God from the book of Revelation:

> Then I saw heaven opened, and behold, a white horse! He who sat upon it is called Faithful and True, and in righteousness he judges and makes war. His eyes are like a flame of fire, and on his head are many diadems; and he has a name inscribed which no one knows but himself. He is clothed in a robe dipped in blood, and the name by which he is called is The Word of God. And the armies of heaven, wearing fine linen, white and pure, followed him on white horses. From his mouth issues a sharp sword with which to strike the nations, and he will rule them with a rod of iron; he will tread the winepress of the fury of the wrath of God the Almighty. On his robe and on his thigh he has a name inscribed, King of kings and Lord of lords. (Rev. 19:11–16)

Young men, even today, are given a holy burden: they are called to wield power and determination righteously. They must learn to do all that is possible and beg for a share of the Spirit (their armor)! Why would we not want them to occupy a place beside the King of kings and the Lord of lords?

This is the Christian man's birthright.

For too long men have been taught to be weak and impotent.

A disciple must claim his God-given power and commit himself to be a champion of the truth. He must defend the Church, his family and friends, and his country. He must live as a warrior, no longer for himself, but for the cause of righteousness, justice, truth, and peace! And that will never happen leaning over a joystick and gazing dumbly at a computer monitor.

The warrior's greatest enemy is apathy.

The world is filled with apathetic men; they are so afraid to fight or have so little interest in what truly matters that the enemy encounters little resistance. While the evils of abortion and pornography and divorce and drug abuse and atheism and materialism slowly choke our society, good men do nothing. The battle escalates, but the soldiers have fled; or, rather, like huddled rabbits, they wait for someone, anyone, to rally them to the cause of good. The disciple must champion the cause of good and commit himself to the battle. When the opportunity to engage comes, a man should not have to think about his abilities. He must act!

The most formidable enemy of a warrior does not necessarily attack him from the outside, but from within. Fear can crush even the most fearsome of warriors, and we allow it much more power in our lives than is necessary. Men fear so many things. Having been hurt, they fear being hurt again; having made a mistake, they fear that others will discover their faults; having experienced loneliness, they fear being alone again; having been disappointed, they fear their own expectations. Most of all, men commonly fear that everyone will discover that they are a fraud. This is an ultimate fear, and it can be crippling.

A man's defense, then, is to embrace the first beatitude, "Blessed are the poor in spirit, for theirs is the kingdom of heaven" (Matt. 5:3). In this beatitude Christ reminds us that our nature is fallen, wounded, and weak. It is, to be realistic, expected that we will fail from time to time. The question is whether we pick ourselves up and try again. Jesus fell three times on the way to Calvary; we, too, must learn to persevere when we fail. Even though society does not understand this, there is no shame in failing, as long as we do not allow the experience to stop us. In the spiritual realm, when we fail and sin, we must confidently seek the mercy of God. What is there, then, to fear?

The Friendship of David

There is much to be learned from a fascinating relationship in the life of David: the friendship he formed with Saul's son, Jonathan. In the passages below, one can see the great love these two men had for one another. To our modern ears, so afraid of sexual implications, the beauty and inspiration of their friendship is lost. But if we read the story with purity of heart, we experience real masculine love; there is nothing immoral or inappropriate about David's relationship with Jonathan.

> When he had finished speaking to Saul, the soul of Jonathan was knit to the soul of David, and Jonathan loved him as his own soul. Then Jonathan made a covenant with David, because he loved him as his own soul. Jonathan stripped himself of the robe that was upon him, and gave it to David, and his armor, and even his sword and his bow and his belt. And David went out and was successful

wherever Saul sent him; so that Saul set him over the men of war. And this was good in the sight of all the people and in the sight of Saul's servants. (1 Sam. 18:2–5)

In this paragraph, we have an excellent example of Jesus' declaration "Greater love has no man than this, that a man lay down his life for his friends" (John 15:13). We see that Jonathan "stripped himself of the robe that was upon him, and gave it to David, and his armor, and even his sword and his bow and his belt." In other words, Jonathan, the son of King Saul and the heir to the throne of his father, abandons everything and, removing the symbols of his princely office, gives them to David! Jonathan is the true hero in this story; recognizing that David's ability and potential surpass his own, he divests himself of his birthright and selflessly empowers his friend to be the future king.

Jesus Christ does the same: He divests himself of His divinity (emptying Himself, as St. Paul says [Phil. 2:7]) and enrobes His disciples, going so far as to make His followers "divine" (cf. 2 Pet. 1:4) — giving them all that He was to inherit in the eternal Kingdom!

If Jonathan considered the potential of David and empowered him to rule, does Jesus not recognize our potential and empower us to rule as well? Thus are friendship and love marked by unreserved emptying and self-giving for the good of the other. This love is as rare today as it is beautiful.

Then, when David's success threatens Saul, Saul seeks to eliminate David:

And Saul spoke to Jonathan his son and to all his servants, that they should kill David. But Jonathan, Saul's son, delighted much in David. And Jonathan told David, "Saul my father seeks to kill you; therefore take heed to yourself in the morning, stay in a secret place and hide yourself; and I will go out and stand beside my father in the field where you are, and I will speak to my father about you; and if I learn anything I will tell you." And Jonathan spoke well of David to Saul his father, and said to him, "Let not the king sin against his servant David; because he has not sinned against you, and because his deeds have been of good service to you; for he took his life in his hand and he slew the Philistine, and the LORD wrought a great victory for all Israel. You saw it, and rejoiced; why then will you sin against innocent blood by killing David without cause?" And Saul listened to the voice of Jonathan; Saul swore, "As the LORD lives, he shall not be put to death." And Jonathan called David, and Jonathan showed him all these things. (1 Sam. 19:1-7)

As the story becomes more intense, Saul's anger increases. Although he lies several times, claiming he will not lay a hand on David, he attempts to kill him at every turn. Jonathan risks his life for the welfare of his friend, almost catching a spear thrown by his father. In doing so, Jonathan betrays not only his father but also his king. He takes great risks to preserve his friend and could easily be accused of treason. David, in turn, promises not to let "the name of Jonathan be cut off from the house of David" (1 Sam. 2:16).

How poor we are today that a man cannot have this type of friendship with another man, or a woman with a woman, or even a man with a woman. Friendship, like love, is impossible without fidelity. How important it is that we relearn the meaning of love.

In our experience as Catholics, we have an ever-present reminder of holy friendship and selfless love: the Eucharist. Is not

the Eucharist the revelation of the love of Jesus Christ and a
pledge of His faithfulness? Having lived His entire life for others
and having emptied Himself entirely on the Cross, does Christ
not continue to give Himself to men (much as Jonathan gave
himself to David), only this time sacramentally? Is not the Eucharist a sign of Christ's willingness to give everything to His
disciples, His beloved friends? Can we not see that Jesus gave
Himself to us in the Eucharist in order that our souls might be
united to His, just as "the soul of Jonathan was knit to the soul
of David"? Will man ever relearn the love and fidelity modeled
for us in Christ?

David the Stalwart King

Then King David went in and sat before the LORD, and
said, "Who am I, O LORD God, and what is my house, that
thou hast brought me thus far? And this was a small thing
in thy eyes, O God; thou hast also spoken of thy servant's
house for a great while to come, and hast shown me future
generations, O LORD God! And what more can David say
to thee for honoring thy servant? For thou knowest thy
servant. For thy servant's sake, O LORD, and according to
thy own heart, thou hast wrought all this greatness, in
making known all these great things. There is none like
thee, O LORD, and there is no God besides thee, according to all that we have heard with our ears. What other
nation on earth is like thy people Israel, whom God went
to redeem to be his people, making for thyself a name for
great and terrible things, in driving out nations before thy
people whom thou didst redeem from Egypt? And thou
didst make thy people Israel to be thy people for ever;
and thou, O LORD, didst become their God. And now,

O LORD, let the word which thou hast spoken concerning thy servant and concerning his house be established forever, and do as thou hast spoken; and thy name will be established and magnified forever, saying, 'The LORD of hosts, the God of Israel, is Israel's God,' and the house of thy servant David will be established before thee. For thou, my God, hast revealed to thy servant that thou wilt build a house for him; therefore thy servant has found courage to pray before thee. And now, O LORD, thou art God, and thou hast promised this good thing to thy servant; now therefore may it please thee to bless the house of thy servant, that it may continue forever before thee; for what thou, O LORD, hast blessed is blessed forever."
(1 Chron. 17:16–27)

For years, we have been taught by Hollywood, those who are allergic to authority, that kings were ruthless, selfish men who took advantage of the people entrusted to them. Of course, these types of kings did exist, but a king was given authority in order to serve his people. It fell to him to provide for defense, to provide food in time of famine, to educate his people, and to keep the peace and be attentive to the common good.

Men are made kings today for the same reason. If the man living in the house at the end of the street is hungry, it is not the sole responsibility of the federal government or the Salvation Army to care for him. That responsibility is also entrusted to you. If drug dealers, thieves, or those given to violence overrun your neighborhood, it is not the sole responsibility of the police department to monitor and correct the situation. That responsibility is also entrusted to you. If a family is poor or homeless, if a boy does not have a father, if the elderly are without resources or assistance, the same can be said. That responsibility is entrusted to you and me. A "successful" king was expected to care for those around him.

Our young men must be taught to do the same. We must remind the disciple to prepare his heart for the mission of the king. He must be the best of kings! A king can be many things: ruler, protector, provider, lawgiver, model, teacher, and mentor. None of this happens without preparation.

My life changed forever when the Dominican sisters in our school sent word home that a family in our parish was desperate for assistance. The father and the mother were both struggling with terminal illnesses. When word reached my parents, they quickly amassed food, clothing, and even toys to be given to this anonymous family.

As a seven-year-old, I was beside myself with selfishness and greed. "Who were my parents," I outrageously thought, "to give food, clothing, and toys to a family other than their own?"

Then the miraculous happened. The day came when Mom told us to load the station wagon with the goods to be donated. When we arrived at the convent, she sent us, arms loaded with packages, to the door (a test of fortitude, if there was one). When the extern sister answered the door, she was overwhelmed by the sight and quickly called the other sisters to their foyer. My siblings and I returned to the car for more packages. When I reentered the foyer of the convent, joyful sisters surrounded us like angels in their Dominican habits, some of them weeping with joy and taking account of all that was donated. The experience changed my life forever. This was the real meaning and purpose of life, and I wanted more. I knew at that moment that, someday and in God's providence, I would be a priest.

In some ways, acquiring the office of king is the pinnacle of a man's life. A man who will be king is endowed by God with power and strength. It remains for him to determine how and for whom that power and strength will be used. A disciple, even now, ought to be in the process of becoming the king God intended. We must never forget: it is God's prerogative to build the Kingdom and to raise the king. As David said, "For thou, my God, hast revealed to thy servant that thou wilt build a house for him; therefore thy servant has found courage to pray before thee." And as David recorded in the psalms, "Unless the LORD build the house, those who build it labor in vain" (127:1). God directs this work. God builds the kingdom, and He builds the king. He—and He alone—will bring it to completion.

In his prayer, the disciple must ask the Lord consistently to prepare him to be king (husband, father, priest, doctor, teacher, coach, public servant, and so forth). He must ask God, again, to heal his heart and to strengthen his body and his resolve. And the mentor must remind him of his confidence and always encourage his dependence on God. He must delight in the disciple as our Heavenly Father delights in him.

But herein lies the problem with men today. A man cannot at the same time be concerned with "little things" (his own needs, material things, his pride or reputation, games—sometimes including sports—money, position, sexual desire, and so on) and have greatness of soul. A small-minded man simply cannot conceive of greatness or of great things.

Our young men have the ability.

As has been said repeatedly, men yearn for greatness, and a young man should not be ashamed of that fact; God bestows this privilege upon men as He did upon David and Josiah and Judas Maccabeus and Peter and Constantine and Leo the Great and St. Louis and Charlemagne and John Paul II and your father, grandfather, uncle, and the man who mentored you.

Developmental Necessity

A magnanimous king is a warrior, a lover, and a sage. He can never doubt that he is a beloved son. And because of all this, he is a man living for and with others. He must freely give himself entirely for God and for the well-being of his brothers and sisters in Christ, and pray God, he makes it happen.

Most young men are intensely aware of their inadequacy in the face of so great a task. A man must make a sensible assessment of his situation. He may feel inadequate or believe he is the wrong man for the job or that he is not up for the challenge. The cross can be heavy, even overwhelming and nearly impossible. But he must always keep his idealism. He will certainly fail at times, but he should be taught to consider failure an education. He will certainly feel inadequate at times, but he must consider inadequacy an invitation to trust. He will undoubtedly feel isolated or alone, but he must consider this an invitation to seek the counsel and friendship of God, of a good man, or both.

David's Prayer of Praise

I will never forget the evening a group of high school men, their chaperones, and I hiked to the top of Hawksbill Mountain in the Shenandoah Mountains. When we arrived at the top, one of the high school men asked if we could pray, so we prayed the Divine Mercy Chaplet. I, awkwardly of course, intoned the chant. After a few chuckles, we figured out the tone and began to settle into the rhythm of prayer. The evening sun was golden, and breathtaking white clouds moved magnificently before an opulent blue sky, so characteristic of these mountains. The Shenandoah Valley stretched for miles north and south, and people in small towns and villages went about their business miles below us. A cool breeze moved among the group.

Suddenly, the chant faltered somewhat at the sound of an animal in the nearby thicket. As the chant continued (even as all eyes looked nervously toward the woods), a young whitetail buck emerged from the woods and fearlessly approached the edge of our group. The symbolism was rich and unforgettable. A young buck, nubs emerging from his head, at the dawn of his prime, stood silently and was content to stand almost majestically before the group. This animal shared so much with the young men in our group. The buck was an iconic symbol of promising male potential. As he stood nearby, he seemed to be present to the prayer, taking it in, and he departed only when we chanted our last amen. The young men remained seated upon the rocky mountaintop for a good hour, silent, peaceful, and contemplative.

> Blessed art thou, O Lord, the God of Israel our father, for ever and ever. Thine, O Lord, is the greatness, and the power, and the glory, and the victory, and the majesty," King David would pray, "for all that is in the heavens and in the earth is thine; thine is the kingdom, O Lord, and thou art exalted as head above all. . . . Honor come[s] from thee, and thou rulest over all. In thy hand are power and might; and in thy hand it is to make great and to give strength to all. And now we thank thee, our God, and praise thy glorious name. (1 Chron. 29:10–13)

Perhaps the young men of our group would be at a loss as to the articulation of such praise, but they surely beheld the spirit. How we shortchange young men and doubt their ability to see beauty, to seek truth, and to enjoy giving praise and glory to the God of the universe. Certainly, young men must be shown or even introduced to such lofty concepts.

Under the guidance of a tough old codger, I once hiked with a group of young men in California. We were enjoying the experience of a Sunday afternoon in the mountains, swimming in a mountain creek, hiking, and napping under ancient mountain trees, which grew twisted and bent by a lifetime of fierce mountain weather. The old man stopped the group, bent down, plucked a tiny mountain flower, and held it between his calloused fingers. He was attempting to make the comparison between the massive mountains that surrounded us and the delicate, miniscule blossom he held in his hand when he was overcome by the wise and creative genius of God. He was unable to talk as tears tracked over his cheeks. The young men looked upon him solemnly and, forgetting the mundane life of the modern American male, venerated the man who stood before them and fell more deeply in love with God.

> I know, my God, that thou triest the heart, and hast pleasure in uprightness; in the uprightness of my heart I have freely offered all these things, and now I have seen thy people, who are present here, offering freely and joyously to thee. O LORD, the God of Abraham, Isaac, and Israel, our fathers, keep forever such purposes and thoughts in the hearts of thy people, and direct their hearts toward thee. (1 Chron. 29:17–18)

In yet another memorable experience, we were enjoying the final day of a perfect fishing trip on a remote lake in Northern Canada. As the sun began to set over the lake, I decided to take a boat for one last trip across the water. A young man in our group elected to join me and positioned himself in the bow of the aluminum fishing boat. Amid bald eagles, loons, massive trees, and dark bluish-gray water, we set out toward the setting sun.

The scene was indescribable, and neither of us uttered a word. As the sun sank below the horizon, the young man raised his hands toward the sky, leaned into the cool Canadian wind, and gave praise to God. He was not necessarily a religious man, but his heart was pierced by the beauty and tender care of the God of the universe. In that moment, the ancient words of a very holy man, St. Augustine, came to mind: "A man's capacity to receive God and hold him fast is that which makes him what he is."

David's Last Instruction to His Son

When David's time to die drew near, he charged his son Solomon: "I am about to go the way of all the earth. Be strong, and show yourself a man, and keep the charge of the LORD your God, walking in his ways and keeping his statutes, his commandments, his ordinances, and his testimonies, as it is written in the law of Moses, that you may prosper in all that you do and wherever you turn; that the LORD may establish his word which he spoke concerning me, saying, 'If your sons take heed to their way, to walk before me in faithfulness with all their heart and with all their soul, there shall not fail you a man on the throne of Israel'" (1 Kings 2:1–4).

Then David said to Solomon, "Be strong and of good courage, and do it. Fear not, be not dismayed; for the LORD God, even my God, is with you. He will not fail you or forsake you, until all the work for the service of the house of the LORD is finished" (1 Chron. 28:20).

There is not much that remains. But the time is now for your disciple to take personal responsibility for his destiny. If he does not strive to be deliberate in his growth, none will occur. You must ask him, "Where are you going? Who will you become? What will you achieve?

Developmental Necessity

As you know, time is not static — it never ceases to pass. When your disciple looks back on his life — back ten, twenty, thirty years — when he looks back to the day he was twelve, sixteen, seventeen, or twenty-five, thirty, or thirty-five years of age, what will be his legacy? What will be his destiny? Today will have an immense impact on thirty years from now. Most men, whether they have failed or succeeded, come out wise in the end. The trials and tests of life can make a boy into a wise man. Very rarely does one find an "unwise" old man.

When David grew old, he passed his kingdom to his chosen son, Solomon. After Solomon was anointed, God promised to grant him whatever he desired, and Solomon chose wisdom. Most have heard of the wisdom of Solomon. In this world, there are two types of people: those who understand and those who do not. There are those for whom the world is a marvelous place to study, learn, and experience, and those who watch television and smoke pot.

Conclusion

THE REWARD AND
ST. AUGUSTINE'S BIRDS

Perhaps some will find what is written here to be inadequate. Some may desire a list such as "Ten Steps Guaranteed to Build a Better Man." Do not be fooled: these types of programs will nearly always fail. In mentoring, we are working with a living human being. Each boy or young man, as the Church teaches, is unique and unrepeatable. Each will bring a new set of circumstances and experiences that must be respected, if not utterly reverenced. Each will have experienced grace and nature in a unique and personal way. Only by entering a trusting and disinterested relationship will a man be able to mentor his disciple or his son effectively.

There is no program; mentoring is based on a sacred relationship. Admittedly, this can be very challenging and sometimes even personally taxing, but, if accomplished with integrity and with the disciple's good always the priority, it will nearly always be successful.

Do not be afraid.

If you are an accomplished man with a lifetime of experiences, you are just the man a boy or a young man needs to achieve human triumphs, personal victories, and, it is hoped, personal sanctity.

Scientists teach us that successful child rearing ends when the offspring reach their own "reproductive success." In other words, a father has been successful when he raises a child until that child can pass his genetic code to the next generation. Mirroring the idea, can we not also say that a mentor is successful when his disciple has reached "human success" and is capable of effectively mentoring the next generation?

The always dependable and incredibly insightful St. Augustine has provided one last meditation for the close of this book. He encouraged parents to imitate the common sparrow. In the course of time, the sparrow finds a partner, mates, lays and incubates a clutch of eggs, and tirelessly spends the summer searching—endlessly back and forth—for food to feed its hungry brood. In the face of danger, the sparrow guards and protects the nest with no regard for its own welfare. Perhaps too soon, the day comes when the young birds take flight and leave the nest, never to be seen again.

Then, as the saint reminds us soberly, the sparrow is satisfied.

Appendix

GUIDELINES FOR YOUNG MEN

I have been invited to speak to many boys and young men during the span of my priesthood. Those audiences are usually the same: a group of half-interested males who have immensely low expectations of guest speakers. After the usual greetings, I often present my "See You on the Other Side List," composed of challenging suggestions that, if taken seriously, can help those boys become good men. I have included the list here with explanatory comments. It is interesting to note that the chaperones and retreat organizers are typically unsettled by the list, but the boys and young men typically respond with keen interest.

Be deliberate.

A boy who seeks to become a man must have a vision of the man he desires to become and must be unquestionably committed to making his vision a reality. This will require sacrifice, work, commitment, and maturity. This work will be completely countercultural, as the culture has a fixation on childhood and desires boys to remain boys as long as possible. A deliberate fellow must weigh every action with the question "Will this help me to realize the vision of the man I seek to be?" If not, it must be abandoned.

Seek God.

God must be the center of a man's life. A man must make friends with God, who is so often seen as an obstacle or a hindrance. It is a man's very destiny and purpose to accomplish God's work and to be with Him forever. Jesus Christ must become his most faithful companion. Otherwise, he will not have the strength and grace he will need to work into the future.

Know your father.

"And he will turn the hearts of fathers to their children and the hearts of children to their fathers" (Mal. 4:6). Every mentor must encourage his disciple to maintain and grow in relationship with his real father. The mentor only endorses and reinforces all that his real father is teaching him—provided the relationship is positive and life giving. Fathers must never question their influence and power in the lives of their sons or begrudge their sons valuable time together.

Find a mentor (a man or men).

A mentor is indispensable to a boy if he is to negotiate the pitfalls and negative influences of today's culture. Youth is a time for learning and defining oneself. This work is more effectively accomplished under the guidance of a connected and influential adult.

Realize the gift of manhood.

Boys have been conditioned to see themselves as problematic and the source of much of what is wrong in the world. On the contrary, boys and young men ought to see manhood as a privilege. They ought to see their manliness as the vehicle by which they will engage the world in order to make significant contributions to their families, communities, church, and world. If adult manhood is not seen as an adventure to be seized (especially for the benefit of others), a young man has not been properly mentored.

Be a gentleman.

Contrary to popular opinion, being a gentleman is not a concept foreign to most boys. They have only to be taught and encouraged. I once wrote a paper for boys on etiquette. A group of mothers ridiculed the effort and were quite surprised to find their sons following the dictates of gentlemanly etiquette.

Do not trust the culture or the political, media, or educational establishments.

I teach my boys to have a "sacred cynicism" about most things, especially things learned in school. Counterproductive and conflicting agendas permeate our lives today. A boy must be able to discern what is good and what is to be avoided.

Expect more of yourself and push yourself (even if those around you do not).

Boys and young men are quite capable of striving for excellence. A mentor can encourage, push, inspire, admonish, and hold a boy or a young man to a higher standard. Boys and young men respond well to such direction. The challenge tells them intuitively, "This man sees that I am worthwhile." Rarely will a disciple refuse the challenge if it is presented well.

Set (major and minor) goals for yourself and strive to reach them.

A boy cannot be expected to reach excellence in a vacuum. Goals keep a boy focused and deliberate. Goals can raise a boy to higher standards and help him arrive at new heights. He must be supervised and must set goals that are both challenging and realizable. Sharing his goals with you will dramatically increase his chances of achieving them. He must also experience the exhilaration of achieving goals (which will motivate him to choose more) and must hear your praise for goals achieved.

Have a desire to learn and seek a classical education.

Local and federal governments fund our educational system. Bureaucrats want one thing in return for educational investments: future taxpayers. Boys should be exposed to poetry, art, and readings in the classics, and should be taught to reason. Even boys who choose vocational pursuits are capable of reading and receiving a classical education. Certainly, a boy or a young man must be convinced of the value found therein; and if he sees that it is important to you and to your development, he will gladly take up the effort.

Read, read, read.

Boys learn to hate reading. Teachers push boys to read when they are too young. They are given cheap reading material or material that appeals only to girls. Give boys books about history, war, great men, and science, and watch the transformation. Boys who learn to love to read will have a distinct advantage over their nonreading peers.

Explore; be curious about the world and everything in it.

A trip to the zoo, a backpacking adventure, a natural history museum, a planetarium, a summer on a farm, woodworking, and other such experiences are powerful enough to open a boy to a marvelous world worth exploring.

Take educated risks and engage in prudent adventures.

Epic adventures (always under your supervision) can impact a boy or a young man greatly. Young people savor adventures. Frustrated once with two seminarians who were content with mediocrity, I ordered them to pack a backpack and spend the summer in Europe. I provided some funds and the instructions to stay out of pubs and bars. On their return, they talked of monasteries, historical churches, castles, battlefields, restaurants, and people, and had endless stories worthy to be told.

Fear drugs and alcohol.

I am honest with young people when I tell them that I never tried drugs because I was intensely afraid I would like them. Asking them to say no is an invitation to explore drugs or underage drinking. Let them know that the day will come when they can drink in moderation as adult men. It could be considered a rite of passage to sit down with you at eighteen and smoke a good cigar or at twenty-one and have an adult beverage. Press upon them the utter stupidity and recklessness of binge drinking. Teach them the military rule (for those over twenty-one): two drinks and you are done.

Do not date until you are twenty-one.

This dictate usually creates a wildly defensive reaction, until you remind a young man that he has nothing to give a young woman — just yet. If he were to ask me for my daughter, I would ask him, "Who do you think you are?" followed by, "Go make something of yourself and then come back and ask again!" This, of course, does not mean they must shun the girls or young women in their lives. But they should be encouraged to go on many dates with different women and none exclusively. Women should be respected, and sexual intimacy should be reserved for marriage. The time to date exclusively comes after the age of twenty-one. The development of so many young men is arrested when they forsake the program in favor of "hanging out" with their girlfriends at the mall.

Choose friends wisely, and don't yield to peer pressure.

Boys should pick friends who are superior to them. This will ensure that time spent together will be productive and challenging. Playing basketball with someone with superior skills serves only to make you better at basketball. Boys should be told that peer pressure is for the weak and characterless. This includes rappers, narcissistic athletes, and countless other childish boys produced by Hollywood.

Respect the automobile.

I have presided at the funerals of three young men killed in automobile accidents. Teach your disciple to respect the automobile.

Avoid pornography at all costs.

Boys must be taught that the pornography industry is sinister and wicked. They may think the activity innocent, but pornographers are looking only to form an addiction in men that will cost huge amounts of money and suffering in the future. It is never free. It is safe to assume that all boys have been exposed to some form of pornography and many languish under the weight of the resulting shame. Delicate and careful instruction (you do not want to teach boys about something they may not yet have experienced) can ease the shame and allow for good and worthy conversation.

Keep sports in perspective.

Sports can consume young people. They are good and worthwhile, but a boy should not live or die by the success he has on the court or on the field. This will not be a popular stand, but when sports replace Sunday Mass, family activities, or other worthwhile pursuits, they need to be curtailed.

Do not play video games.

The dictate not to play video games is never popular among young men, and you must be convincing about it. Video games don't contribute to one's success or character as a man. If some will not hear it, so be it, but the others have more important work to accomplish.

Limit the use of technology (texting, IM, Netflix, e-mail, Facebook, the Internet).

Soon the culture will learn that solid relationships and real friendships are not supported by technology. Perhaps technology is unavoidable, but it is to the detriment of our humanity to be consumed by technology. Ironically, boys and young men are aware of this, as well as the detrimental effects of video games, and may need only your reasoning to help convince them.

Learn a foreign language, a musical instrument, a trade, or a skill.

Why not? These activities are more easily learned the younger one begins. They are skills that will be valuable and useful for a man's entire life.

*Learn to be a leader and
prepare with an eye to the future.*

This dictate will take a boy or a young man into a valuable and worthwhile future. If he is to be someone worthy to contend with, it begins long before he reaches mature manhood.

* * *

Of course, all these directives will require your convincing and uncompromising encouragement. Again, you will not succeed in convincing anyone of the merits found here if you yourself are not living well. Personal integrity is a prerequisite for raising the prospect of the challenges found here. Do not be afraid to challenge young men with well-reasoned and dispassionate arguments. They will surely listen.

BIBLIOGRAPHY

Airaksinen, Toni. "Princeton's New 'Men's Engagement Manager' to Combat Aggressive Masculinity on Campus." The College Fix, July 25, 2017. https://www.thecollegefix.com/post/34858/.

American Psychiatric Association. *Diagnostic and Statistical Manual of Mental Disorders*. 4th ed. Washington, D.C.: American Psychiatric Association, 2000.

Aquinas, Thomas. *Commentary on Aristotle's Nicomachean Ethics*. Translated by C. I. Litzinger. Notre Dame, IN: Dumb Ox Books, 1964.

———. *Summa Theologica*, IIa-IIae, QQ. 1–148. Translated by the Fathers of the English Dominican Province. Allen, TX: Christian Classics, 1981.

Auerbach, Carl F., and Louise B. Silverstein. "Deconstructing the Essential Father." *American Psychologist* 54, no. 6 (1999): 397–407.

Augustine of Hippo. *The Confessions*. Translated by Maria Boulding. Hyde Park, NY: New City Press, 1997.

Baars, Conrad. *Born Only Once: The Miracle of Affirmation.* Quincy, IL: Franciscan Herald Press, 1975.

Baumeister, Roy F. *Is There Anything Good about Men? How Cultures Flourish by Exploiting Men.* NY: Oxford University Press, 2010.

Benedict XVI. General Audience, June 27, 2012.

Bergamo, Cajetan de. *Humility of Heart.* New York: Veritatis Splendor Publications, 2012.

Bergsma, John. *The Dead Sea Scrolls and the Jewish Roots of the Church.* 18 CDs. New Orleans, LA: Catholic Productions, n.d.

Boteach, Rabbi Shmuley. *The Broken American Male and How to Fix Him.* New York: St. Martin's Press, 2008.

Campbell, Olivia. "The Men Taking Classes to Unlearn Toxic Masculinity." *The Cut,* October 23, 2017. https://www.the-cut.com/2017/10/the-men-taking-classes-to-unlearn-toxic-masculinity.html.

Catechism of the Catholic Church. Vatican City: Libreria Editrice Vaticana, 1992.

Catholic News Service. "Body Found of 24-Year-Old Seminarian Who Drowned." *Catholic Herald,* August 4, 2016. http://catholicherald.co.uk/news/2016/08/04/body-found-of-24-year-old-seminarian-who-drowned/.

Christoff, Matthew J. *The New Emangelization: The Catholic "Man-Crisis" Fact Sheet.* The New Emangelization, July 7, 2015. http://www.newemangelization.com/man-crisis/the-catholic-man-crisis-factsheet/.

Congressional Budget Office. *Trends in the Joblessness and Incarceration of Young Men*. Congressional Budget Office, May 9, 2016. http://www.cbo.gov/publication/51495.

Corneau, Guy. *Absent Fathers, Lost Sons: The Search for Masculine Identity*. Boston: Shambhala, 1991.

Cross, Gary. *Men to Boys: The Making of Modern Immaturity*. New York: Columbia University Press, 2008.

Curtin, Sally C., Margaret Warner, and Holly Hedegaard. *Suicide Rates for Females and Males by Race and Ethnicity: United States, 1999 and 2014*. Washington, D.C.: National Center for Health Statistics, 2016. https://www.cdc.gov/nchs/data/hestat/suicide/rates_1999_2014.pdf.

Daniélou, Jean. *The Lord of History: Reflections on the Inner Meaning of History*. Translated by Nigel Abercrombie. London: Longmans, Green, 1958.

Duke Women's Center. Duke Men's Project. Facebook Page. https://www.facebook.com/pg/DukeMensProject/about/?ref=page_internal.

Edsall, Thomas B. "The Increasing Significance of the Decline of Men." *New York Times*, March 16, 2017.

Eldredge, John. *The Way of the Wild Heart: A Map for the Masculine Journey*. Nashville: Thomas Nelson, 2006.

Eschner, Kat. "Three New Things Science Says about Dads." Smithsonian.com, June 16, 2017, http://www.smithsonianmag.com/smart-news/three-new-things-science-says-about-dads-180963698/.

Fitzgibbons, Richard, and Joseph Nicolosi. "When Boys Won't Be Boys: Childhood Gender Identity Disorder." *Lay Witness*

(June 2001). Posted at Catholic Education Resource Center. https://www.catholiceducation.org/en/marriage-and-family/sexuality/when-boys-won-t-be-boys-childhood-gender-indentity-disorder.html.

Franklin, Karen. "Inside the Mind of People Who Hate Gays." *Frontline Newsletter*, 2016. https://www.pbs.org/wgbh/pages/frontline/shows/assault/roots/franklin.html.

French, David. "On Man's Duty to Defend the Weak and Vulnerable." *National Review*, July 15, 2015. http://www.nationalreview.com/article/421227/mans-duty-defend-weak-and-vulnerable-david-french.

Hahn, Andrew. "New Campus Program Asks, 'What Is Masculinity?'" University of Wisconsin–Madison, University Health Services. https://www.uhs.wisc.edu/news/campus/mens-project/.

Havard, Alexandre. *Created for Greatness: The Power of Magnanimity*. New Rochelle, NY: Scepter Press, 2014.

Hoff Sommers, Christina. *The War Against Boys: How Misguided Policies Are Harming Our Young Men*. New York: Simon and Schuster, 2013.

———. "School Has Become Too Hostile to Boys." *Time*, August 19, 2013. http://ideas.time.com/2013/08/19/school-has-become-too-hostile-to-boys/

Hymowitz, Kay S. "Where Have the Good Men Gone?" *Wall Street Journal*, February 19, 2011. Posted at Catholic Education Resource Center. http://www.catholiceducation.org/en/controversy/marriage/where-have-the-good-men-gone.html.

————. *Manning Up: How the Rise of Women Has Turned Men into Boys*. New York: Basic Books, 2012.

Ingalhalikar, Madhura, Alex Smith, Drew Parker, Theodore D. Satterthwaite, Mark A. Elliott, Kosha Ruparel, Hakon Hakonarson, Raquel E. Gur, Ruben C. Gur, and Ragini Verma. *Sex Differences in the Structural Connectome of the Human Brain*. Edited by Charles Gross. *PNAS* 111, no. 2 (January 14, 2014): 823–828. http://www.pnas.org/content/111/2/823.

John Paul II. *Crossing the Threshold of Hope*. New York: Alfred A. Knopf, 1994.

————. Encyclical letter *Redemptor Hominis*. March 4, 1979. http://w2.vatican.va/content/john-paul-ii/en/encyclicals/documents/hf_jp-ii_enc_04031979_redemptor-hominis.html.

Kay, Barbara. "Fictional Drivel." *National Post*, April 14, 2010. Reprinted as "Male Studies: A Proposed Curriculum" at Catholic Education Resource Center. https://www.catholiceducation.org/en/controversy/feminism/male-studies-a-proposed-curriculum.html.

Keating, Michael. "The Strange Case of the Self-Dwarfing Man: Modernity, Magnanimity, and Thomas Aquinas." *Logos* 10, no. 4 (2007): 55–76.

Kullman, Sean. "Invitation to a Dialogue: Helping Boys Succeed" (letter to the editor). *New York Times*, February 23, 2015.

Langbert, Mitchell, Anthony J. Quain, and Daniel Klein. "Faculty Voter Registration in Economics, History, Journalism, Law, and Psychology." *Econ Journal Watch* 13, no. 3 (2017): 422–451.

Maltz, Wendy. "Pornography on the Rise: A Growing Mental Health Problem." *Psychotherapy Networker*, November 11, 2015. https://www.psychotherapynetworker.org/blog/details/677/pornography-on-the-rise-a-growing-mental-health-problem.

Meeker, Meg, M.D. *Strong Fathers, Strong Daughters: Ten Secrets Every Father Should Know*. Washington, D.C.: Regnery Publishing, 2006.

Meyer, Robert, trans. *Palladius: The Lausiac History*. New York: Paulist Press, 1964.

Miner, Brad. *The Compleat Gentleman: The Modern Man's Guide to Chivalry*. Dallas: Spence Publishing, 2004.

Moynihan, Carolyn. "Father's Day: The Difference a Dad Makes." Mercatornet, June 19, 2015. https://www.mercatornet.com/family_edge/view/fathers-day-the-difference-a-dad-makes/16378.

Murphy, Meg. "NowUKnow: Why Millennials Refuse to Get Married." Bentley University, 2017. https://www.bentley.edu/impact/articles/nowuknow-why-millennials-refuse-get-married.

National Center for Education Statistics. (2004). *Trends in Education Equity for Girls and Women*. Washington, D.C.: U.S. Government Printing Office, 2004.

Noone, Gabrielle. "38 Percent of College Men Admit to Coercing Women into Sex, according to a New Study." *New York Magazine* (June 2016). https://www.thecut.com/2016/06/college-men-coercive-sex-study.html.

Bibliography

Olivas, Melissa, Nikki Liu, and Lauren Wallitsch. "The Study of Men and Sexual Addictions." *Psychology of Men* (Fall 2008). https://psychofmen.wordpress.com/final-papers/the-study-of-men-and-sexual-addictions/.

Perry, Mark. "Women Earned Majority of Doctoral Degrees in 2016." *AEIdeas* (blog), September 28, 2017. http://www.aei.org/publication/women-earned-majority-of-doctoral-degrees-in-2016-for-8th-straight-year-and-outnumber-men-in-grad-school-135-to-100/.

Ratzinger, Joseph Cardinal. *Principles of Catholic Theology: Building Stones for a Fundamental Theology*. San Francisco: Ignatius Press, 1987.

Reilly, P. J. "Are Catholic Colleges Leading Students Astray?" *Catholic World Report* (March 2003): 38–47.

Rhoades, Steven E. *Taking Sex Differences Seriously*. San Francisco: Encounter Books, 2004.

Rosin, Hannah. *The End of Men: And the Rise of Women*. New York: Riverhead Books, 2012.

Sax, Leonard, M.D., Ph.D. *Why Gender Matters: What Parents and Teachers Need to Know about the Emerging Science of Sex Differences*. New York: Three Rivers Press, 2005.

———. *Boys Adrift; The Five Factors Driving the Growing Epidemic of Unmotivated Boys and Underachieving Young Men*. New York: Basic Books, 2007.

Siebel Newsom, Jennifer. "The Mask You Live In." Kickstarter, 2016. http://www.kickstarter.com/projects/jensiebelnewsom/the-mask-you-live-in.

Statistica. "U.S. Homosexuality: Statistics and Facts." Statistica, 2017. https://www.statista.com/topics/1249/homosexuality/.

Smith, Helen, Ph.D. *Men on Strike: Why Men Are Boycotting Marriage, Fatherhood, and the American Dream — and Why It Matters.* New York: Encounter Books, 2013.

Smith, Kyle. "Life in the Childish States of America." *New York Post*, May 29, 2016. https://nypost.com/2016/05/29/life-in-the-childish-states-of-america/.

Sossamon, Jeff. "Girls Lead Boys in Academic Achievement Globally." News Bureau, University of Missouri–Columbia, January 26, 2015. http://munews.missouri.edu/news-releases/2015/0126-girls-lead-boys-in-academic-achievement-globally/.

Stenson, James. "Danger Signs: Families Headed for Trouble." Catholic Parents OnLine, 2005. https://www.catholicparents.org/danger-signs-families-headed-trouble/

Tilghman, Andrew. "The Military May Relax Recruiting Standards for Fitness and Pot Use." *Military Times*, November 1, 2016.

van den Aardweg, Gerard. "On the Psychogenesis of Homosexuality." *Linacre Quarterly* 78, no. 3 (2011): 330–354.

Vespa, Jonathan. *The Changing Economics and Demographics of Young Adulthood: 1975–2016.* Publication no. P20-579. Washington, D.C.: United States Census Bureau, 2017. https://www.census.gov/content/dam/Census/library/publications/2017/demo/p20-579.pdf.

von Balthasar, Hans Urs. *Love Alone Is Credible.* San Francisco: Ignatius Press, 2004.

Bibliography

Ward, Benedicta, trans. *The Wisdom of the Desert Fathers*. Oxford, England: SLG Press, 1981.

Weigel, George. *Witness to Hope: The Biography of Pope John Paul II*. New York: HarperCollins, 1999.

White, Doug and Polly. "What to Expect from Gen-X and Millennial Employees." *Entrepreneur*, December 23, 2014. https://www.entrepreneur.com/article/240556.

Wilson, Derek. *Charlemagne: A Biography*. New York: Doubleday, 2006.

For more information on the work of mentoring or to ask Fr. Peter Henry a question, please write to him at fatherpetermhenry@gmail.com.

Sophia Institute

Sophia Institute is a nonprofit institution that seeks to nurture the spiritual, moral, and cultural life of souls and to spread the Gospel of Christ in conformity with the authentic teachings of the Roman Catholic Church.

Sophia Institute Press fulfills this mission by offering translations, reprints, and new publications that afford readers a rich source of the enduring wisdom of mankind.

Sophia Institute also operates two popular online Catholic resources: CrisisMagazine.com and CatholicExchange.com.

Crisis Magazine provides insightful cultural analysis that arms readers with the arguments necessary for navigating the ideological and theological minefields of the day. *Catholic Exchange* provides world news from a Catholic perspective as well as daily devotionals and articles that will help you to grow in holiness and live a life consistent with the teachings of the Church.

In 2013, Sophia Institute launched Sophia Institute for Teachers to renew and rebuild Catholic culture through service to Catholic education. With the goal of nurturing the spiritual, moral, and cultural life of souls, and an abiding respect for the role and work of teachers, we strive to provide materials and programs that are at once enlightening to the mind and ennobling to the heart; faithful and complete, as well as useful and practical.

Sophia Institute gratefully recognizes the Solidarity Association for preserving and encouraging the growth of our apostolate over the course of many years. Without their generous and timely support, this book would not be in your hands.

www.SophiaInstitute.com
www.CatholicExchange.com
www.CrisisMagazine.com
www.SophiaInstituteforTeachers.org

Sophia Institute Press® is a registered trademark of Sophia Institute.
Sophia Institute is a tax-exempt institution as defined by the
Internal Revenue Code, Section 501(c)(3). Tax I.D. 22-2548708.